The Modern Idea
of History and its Value

The Modern Idea of History and its Value

An Introduction by
Chiel van den Akker

AUP

Original title *Geschiedenis*
First published in 2019 by Athenaeum – Polak & Van Gennep, Amsterdam
Copyright © 2019 by Chiel van den Akker
Chapter 6: © C. van den Akker / Amsterdam University Press B.V.,
Amsterdam 2020

Cover illustration: Nicolas Poussin, *A Dance to the Music of Time*,
c. 1634-1636. Via Wikimedia Commons. © Public Domain

Cover design:
Lay-out: Crius Group, Hulshout

ISBN   978 94 6372 833 1
e-ISBN   978 90 4855 205 4
NUR   687

Table of Contents

Preface

This short book aims to answer two questions: What is history? And what is its value? It also attempts to show how the answers to these questions are mutually dependent. Think for instance of the old view that history is the teacher of life. This view assumes that the past is a reservoir of examples from which moral lessons for the present can be drawn. If one attempts to theorize what history is, one immediately moves on to speculating what history is for.

I am not the first to ask these questions. This book discusses the answers of a select group of influential historians and philosophers. These individuals were chosen for their inspiring and influential views on history and its value. I will set them in conversation with one another and show how their views are still relevant today.

Mostly, I will focus on the modern idea of history and its criticism. The ancient Greeks' conception of history is, however, an indispensable part of both. The modern idea of history is the product of the nineteenth century, when history solidified as an academic discipline and philosophers posited the idea that the course of history is intelligible.

I hope this short book will stimulate readers to think about their idea of history and its usefulness. I also hope that they will look with fresh eyes at the histories that are told today. This book is meant for anyone with an interest in the concept of history and its value, and it is especially intended for students of history.

At the end of this book, the reader will find an overview of the sources on which each chapter draws and an index. I also provide a list of recommended – mostly recent – readings for those who want to look further into the subjects this book touches upon.

Acknowledgements

This book is a revised edition and translation of my Dutch book *Geschiedenis* in the series *Elementaire Deeltjes*, which was published by Athenaeum in Amsterdam in 2019. Chapter 6 is newly written for this book. I am very grateful to Daniel Woolf for correcting the English of my manuscript and for his many helpful suggestions.

Chapter 2 quotes from Thucydides, *On Justice, Power, and Human Nature. The Essence of Thucydides' History of the Peloponnesian War*, edited and translated by Paul Woodruff, © Hackett Publishing 1993. These quotes are reprinted by permission of Hackett Publishing Company, Inc. All rights reserved. The same publisher also gave permission to use quotes from Nietzsche's *On the Advantage and Disadvantage of History for Life*, which was translated by Peter Preuss and published in 1980.

1.   The Value of History for Life

The title of this first chapter refers to the 1874 essay *Vom Nutzen und Nachteil der Historie für das Leben* by the German philologist Friedrich Nietzsche (1844–1900). History, Nietzsche claimed, is to serve life. This was not a new claim; to the contrary. Nietzsche himself points to the Greek historian Polybius (c. 200–120), whose work on the Roman Empire starts with the comment that there is no better guide to life than knowledge of the past. He says:

> Polybius, for example, calls political history the proper preparation for governing a state and the great teacher who, by reminding us of the sudden misfortunes of others, exhorts us steadfastly to bear the reverses of fortune. (p. 15)

In his essay, Nietzsche is not interested in political history. He is also not solely concerned with 'men of action', as was Polybius, who wrote his history with the politicians and military leadership of the Roman Empire in mind. But everyone benefits from history according to Polybius, as Nietzsche emphasizes, for history teaches us how to bear the vicissitudes of fortune.

The idea that history is the teacher of life is an old one. It is typical of the so-called exemplary history which was dominant from Roman antiquity to the nineteenth century. The past offered *exempla* ('examples') of behaviour from which political and moral lessons could be drawn. Think for instance of the following advice offered by Polybius:

> It is of the greatest importance for statesmen to make sure that they understand the true reasons whereby old enmities are

reconciled or new friendships formed. They should observe when it is that men come to terms because they are yielding to circumstances, and when because their spirit has been broken. (III.11)

Given the examples it could provide, the past also served a function in speeches: An orator could use examples from the past to give authority and credibility to his arguments – and to entertain his audience, as the Roman politician and orator Marcus Tullius Cicero (106–143) added. For a historian such as Polybius, such a rhetorical use of history was far removed from the kind of work he did as a historian. But for him, too, history had a didactic function. It was political and moral instruction: Philosophy teaching by example, and as such was a guide to life.

While others in the nineteenth century would reject exemplary history (a point we will come back to later), Nietzsche gives it his own twist. He also emphasizes that while history can be useful, it may also be an obstacle to life. He warns us of having too much history. An excess of history was, Nietzsche believed, a problem in the nineteenth century. Never before had there been so much knowledge of the past available. Man had to carry an evergrowing past along with him.

The answer to what history *is* provides an answer to what its *use* is and vice versa. This is evident in the old view that history is political and moral instruction using past examples. When preparing for a political career, it is good to know how to conclude treaties and wage wars, and what personality traits are required for these activities. It is also good to have knowledge of the various forms of government, and how they are subject to change. The interdependence between the two questions is nowhere as clear as in Nietzsche's essay. That is why this book starts with him.

In his essay, Nietzsche distinguishes between three kinds of history: the monumental, the antiquarian, and the critical. They are respectively concerned with the person who acts and strives for something, the person who wants to preserve and venerate the past, and the person who suffers and seeks liberation from it. Each kind of history may serve life and is useful in its own right. A balance must therefore be struck between these kinds of history. Nietzsche puts it thus:

> If the man who wants to achieve something great needs the past at all he will master it through monumental history; who on the other hand likes to persist in the traditional and venerable will care for the past as an antiquarian historian; and only he who is oppressed by some present misery and wants to throw off the burden at all cost has a need for critical, that is judging and condemning history. (pp. 18–19)

With these distinctions, Nietzsche reverts to older kinds of history that had fallen into disuse in the nineteenth century among academically trained historians and other scholars. He does, however, offer his own interpretation of the terms he uses, thereby giving them a broader meaning.

The antiquarian historical sense is for people who cherish traditions. Such people feel connected to their environment and the customs that are common there. They value an heirloom because it is part of their family history. A parent's diary is retained because they recognize themselves in the life it describes. The simple rural life is appreciated because that life has been lived there for centuries. Walking down a city street evokes the feeling of kinship with previous residents. And when they hear the national anthem being played, they feel connected to their fatherland. Nietzsche writes:

> This antiquarian historical sense of reverence is of highest value where it imbues modest, coarse, even wretched conditions in which a man or a people live with a simple touching feeling of pleasure and contentment. (pp. 19–20)

Antiquarian history shows that the life we're living is not accidental and random: It has grown that way historically. Feeling connected with the past – with our heritage – and cherishing that connection reassures us. This is how antiquarian history serves life.

The antiquarian historical sense is not without its dangers. The danger is that everything that is old is perceived as equally venerable, simply because it is old, and all the new is rejected, because it cannot be better than the old. Life is only preserved, even mummified, in antiquarian history. The past continuously offers itself for comparison, giving us the feeling that we are but descendants and epigones, and that the present has nothing to offer. At such a moment, the past has become a burden:

> Then you may well witness the repugnant spectacle of a blind lust for collecting, of a restless raking together of all that once has been. (p. 21)

The antiquarian historical sense acquires a systematic meaning in Nietzsche's essay. The desire to hold on to the past by preserving it, and the veneration of what is old, are phenomena of all times and places.[1]

Nietzsche concludes that the antiquarian historical sense cannot generate life. It can only preserve it. That is why we need the two other kinds of history.

Sometimes we have to be critical of the past and condemn it. Such is the case when the past is experienced as a burden and we wonder how we can organize life in such a way that we are freed from that burden. This is how the critical sense of history serves life. For this critical sense, a person

> must have the strength, and use it from time to time, to shatter and dissolve something to enable him to live: this he achieves by dragging it to the bar of judgment, interrogating it meticulously and finally condemning it. (pp. 21–22)

Here, Nietzsche is concerned with human errors and forms of injustice that deserve to be banished. He gives as an example the privileges possessed by some historical groups and points to the systems of castes and dynasties. Today, we would include in this consideration such historical phenomena as slavery, colonialism, the inequality between men and women, and racism.

---

1   It should be noted that antiquarianism has an additional historical meaning, though not one that interested Nietzsche. It has commonly been used to describe the activities of early modern collectors of plants, minerals, books, medals, coins, ancient manuscripts, and scientific instruments, and their preference for the curious, obscure, and particular. The antiquarian was often contrasted with the historian: The antiquarian *collects*, makes inventories, and systematizes his findings, but he does not *select*, as the historian does. Nor does the antiquarian, unlike the historian, use a chronological framework to interpret his objects.

But critical history, too, is not without its dangers, as Nietzsche points out:

> If we condemn those aberrations and think ourselves quite exempt from them, the fact that we are descended from them is not eliminated. (p. 22)

The temptation is strong to appropriate, in retrospect, a past from which we *want* to descend, instead of accepting the past from which we actually descended. No matter how often we condemn slavery and colonialism or reject racism and gender inequality, they remain part of the history that made us ínto who we are.

Thirdly, in addition to the antiquarian and critical kinds of history, Nietzsche discusses monumental history. This is the variety of history which reminds us that great things were possible in the past and that what was once done remains possible both now and in the future. This is how the monumental historical sense serves life. Nietzsche writes that this kind of history is for people who need models and teachers that they cannot find among their contemporaries. It gives strength to the person who wants to accomplish something great:

> And yet time and again some awaken who, in viewing past greatness and strengthened by their vision, rejoice as though human life were a grand affair and as though it were even the sweetest fruit of this bitter growth to know that at some earlier time someone went through existence proud and strong, another in profound thought, a third helpfully and with pity. (pp. 15–16)

The monumental kind of history points us to an inspirational past. It has this in common with the old exemplary history discussed earlier. We must indulge ourselves in Plutarch (c. 46–120), Nietzsche writes, in order that we believe in ourselves by believing in his heroes. (The Greek historian Plutarch is known for his dramatized biographies of distinguished Greeks and Romans in which he harmonizes different character types and their behaviours.)

Once again, however, this kind of history is not without its dangers. The first of these is that the specific circumstances of the great achievements in the past and their specific consequences are forgotten. A second is that the past in a monumental history may be represented more ideally than it actually was, risking transforming it from history into mere fiction. A third danger is that those parts of the past that were not great are neglected or forgotten. Finally, the analogies between the past and the present that the monumental historical sense suggests can be misleading. These analogies encourage overconfidence and fanaticism, and can lead to a misguided heroism in the present. In short, monumental history easily results in a glorification of the past for which the past itself provides no justification. The Dutch Golden Age is undoubtedly a high point in history. But that is no reason for that period to be glorified and presented more ideally than it in fact was. Its dark sides were numerous.

Nietzsche's distinction between the antiquarian, monumental, and critical kinds of history remains of use today, over a century after his death. It enables us to subdivide history into various categories and identify the pros and cons of each. History is of use to people who want to preserve and admire the past, to those who act and strive for something, and to those who suffer and seek liberation from a past that haunts them.

Nietzsche also uses the distinction between the different kinds of history to determine how historians and other scholars should study the past. We will now turn our attention to this.

At first glance, one would think that the critical historical sense is most suited to describe the work of Nietzsche himself. He saw his task as a philologist to be critical of the modern age in which he lived. History had, during the nineteenth century, become an academic discipline, and people were inclined to regard life as thoroughly historical. Everything was *becoming* and also had a history. Later in his essay, however, it becomes clear that Nietzsche prefers the monumental historical sense (this is also apparent from his work on the first Greek philosophers, which he finished in 1873, a year before his *Vom Nutzen und Nachteil*). He states that this kind of history focuses on the best specimens of man (I noted above that monumental history is reminiscent of exemplary history). In such specimens, even the purpose of humanity as a whole is to be found! They provide us with the strength and inspiration to do great things in our own time. It is therefore the task of historical studies to establish a conversation between geniuses. Nietzsche says the following about this:

> These [geniuses] do not, as it were, continue a process but live in timeless simultaneity, thanks to history, which permits such co-operation, they live as the republic of geniuses of which Schopenhauer speaks somewhere. (p. 53)

Elsewhere in his essay, but in this context, he refers to Barthold Georg Niebuhr (1776–1831), the first history professor at the modern University of Berlin, founded in 1810. History, Niebuhr said, when

> clearly and explicitly comprehended, has at least this one use: that one knows how even the greatest and highest spirits of humanity do not know how accidentally their vision adopted the form through which they see and through which they vehemently insist that everyone else see; vehemently that is, since the intensity of their consciousness is exceptionally great. (p. 12)

A great and exalted mind has us look at the world differently. This is what makes his work useful for life. Nietzsche would emphasize that the work of a genius is not merely a product of its time; we should not reduce such a work to its time by taking it to be simply the result of certain circumstances or developments. What is great is immortal, eternal, and therefore superhistorical.

Elsewhere in his essay, Nietzsche criticizes the usual working method of the academic historian: Instead of providing insight into the timelessness of the work of a genius, the historian places that work in a broader context; or he compares it with other, earlier works; or he diverts attention from the work itself by focusing on the influences or circumstances that made it possible; or he analyses it in such a way that it disintegrates into its analysed parts, as a result of which the wholeness of the work, and therefore the work itself, is lost. These are real dangers, which 21st century technology has magnified. Think of art historians who use modern techniques to look through the layers of paint in a painting and believe that what they find there is just as interesting as the painting itself. Or think of scholars who use digital techniques to analyse Shakespeare's corpus without ever reading an actual sonnet or attending a performance of one of his plays. In both cases, the research ignores the genius of the work, which can only be found in the way it changes our view of the world.

It should be noted that when Nietzsche points to the highest specimens of man he is not primarily thinking of politicians and military strategists, as was customary in exemplary history. To the contrary, he has in mind poets, artists, historians, and philosophers, men such as Goethe, Raphael, Thucydides, and Herakleitos. Or, to stay with our earlier example of the Dutch Golden Age, the likes of Vondel, Rembrandt, De Groot, and Spinoza, whose genius is what made that era both great and inspiring.

Nietzsche thus raises the suspicion of advocating a kind of alternative 'great man theory of history': One populated not by generals and politicians, but by scholars and artists. (The idea that all history is political history and concerned with politicians, their personalities, the decisions they made, and the elites to which they belonged, would itself become less and less self-evident in the course of the 20th century). His call to the historian to constitute a republic of geniuses offers a model for intellectual history. Yet, as we will see, Nietzsche does not exclusively advocate for this history of great minds and their creations.

A central criticism in Nietzsche's essay is that the question of how history serves life falls outside the scope of the positivist, who wants to turn history into a science. The term 'positivism' stems from Auguste Comte (1798–1857), who intended by it the scientific approach of social reality. In the context of history as an academic discipline, positivism means two things. The positivist either merely sticks to the facts ('doing justice to the facts' is, according to Nietzsche, a typical German expression). Or he wants to transform history into social science, in line with the model offered by the natural sciences, and to discover the general laws that govern societies. The latter is what Comte had in mind. But, according to Nietzsche, historical studies should not look for general laws of human behaviour. At their best, these show how uniform and dependent the masses are, while what is interesting always rises above the masses. He writes:

> I hope that history may not see its significance in general thoughts as a kind of bloom and fruit: rather that its value is just this, to describe with insight a known, perhaps common theme, an everyday melody, to elevate it, raise to a comprehensive symbol and so let a whole world of depth of meaning, power and beauty be guessed in it. (p. 36)

Nietzsche not only makes this remark in the context of criticizing the idea of turning historical studies into a social science modelled on the natural sciences but also underlines his preference for the monumental conception of history *and* the importance of the personality of the historian.

> If you have not had some higher and greater experiences than all others you will not know how to interpret anything great and high in the past. (p. 38)

Only the great achievements of the past are worth knowing and preserving. The historian must be trained in such a way that he understands that. Once again, it becomes clear that the question of what history *is* – the description of everyday themes from the past and their depths of meaning, power, and beauty – can be directly linked to the question of its *usefulness*: History inspires us and provides insight that makes us look at reality in a different way. The answer to one question leads directly to an answer to the other.

In his essay, Nietzsche turns against his own time and calls his essay *untimely*. The need for history was strong in the nineteenth century, too strong according to Nietzsche. The French politician and historian Prosper de Barante (1782–1866) had even spoken of a historical fever in his 1828 essay 'De l'Histoire'. Nietzsche made the same diagnosis later that century but would, in contrast to Barante, regard it as dangerous and propose three remedies for this illness.

One remedy for an excess of history is simply to *forget*. Forgetting allows one to feel unhistorical and to hold on to the present moment instead of seeing a world that is merely in a state of *becoming*. However, forgetting everything is not an option; then we would also forget everything that makes us human. A past that keeps on forcing itself upon us as comparison and therefore is a burden is best *condemned* – this is the second remedy that Nietzsche offers. His third solution is to focus on the superhistorical: on the eternal that transcends the temporal, on the unchanging, instead of on that which is becoming in time. And then Nietzsche, like his friend the historian Jacob Burckhardt (1818–1897), thinks of art and religion, which give existence an unchanging and eternal character, the work of geniuses, and the power, wisdom, and beauty of everyday life. This third remedy leads to the monumental sense of history preferred by Nietzsche. What is beautiful, wise, powerful, and the product of genius does not belong to a certain time – it is not the product of it – but must be elevated above it. Only what is great in the past is worth knowing and preserving.

Because Nietzsche turns against his own time, he in effect returns to earlier, pre-modern views of history. The claim that only what was great in the past is worth preserving and knowing is one such view. The first historians in antiquity were already of that opinion, which we will discuss further in the next chapter. This theme also resonated at the beginning of the nineteenth century for the aforementioned Niebuhr (incidentally, one of the two nineteenth-century historians mentioned by name by Nietzsche, and the only one quoted with approval). In his history of Rome, Niebuhr had said that he would exclude from what the Romans themselves had written down that which was not great in itself and was without important consequences.

To the extent that this conception of greatness is reminiscent of the exemplary theory of history, it would have been rejected by Niebuhr and other historians of the early nineteenth century. They were particularly interested in the effects that actions and events would have in later times: Those effects were what revealed their greatness. However, nearer the end of the century, Nietzsche would, in his own way, argue for the monumental historical sense, which involves the things that are great in themselves, and not the processes and developments to which they contribute, nor their important consequences.

Nietzsche also discusses themes to which later authors would return, sometimes as a result of his work. The question whether history is or should be a science is one such theme. This theme will be discussed several times throughout this book. In line with this, Nietzsche's essay raises the question whether the subjectivity of the historian – his personality and presence in his work – is something positive. Shouldn't the historian be objective and erase his (subjective) personality from his work as much as possible? Chapter 5 deals with this issue. In this short book, I will point out Nietzsche's influence on later scholars a number of times.

Nietzsche called his reflection on the value and dangers of history for life untimely. He does admit that he is a child of his time, but he is, above all, he says, a student of the ancient Greeks, with whom he felt a close bond. In particular, Nietzsche related most closely to the historian Thucydides (c. 460–400), because of the genuine realism that characterizes the latter's work. In Nietzsche's mind, it is the work of a genius. Nietzsche's admiration for Thucydides was in this instance not 'untimely', at least not among historians. In the nineteenth century, the Greek's history of the Peloponnesian War served as a model for history-writing as it developed into an autonomous academic discipline. It was commonly held that anyone who wanted to know what history is should begin with Thucydides, the *verissimo historiae parenti*: the true father of history, as the lawyer Jean Bodin (1530–1596) had written as far back as the sixteenth century. The next chapter will argue that both Bodin and Nietzsche were right.

2.   The First Historian

At the start of his book on the war between Athens and
Sparta, the Athenian Thucydides (referring to himself in
the third person) makes it clear why he wrote his history:

> He began to write as soon as the war was afoot, with the expec-
> tation that it would turn out to be a great one and that, more
> than all earlier wars, this one would deserve to be recorded.
> He made this prediction because both sides were at their peak
> in every sort of preparation for war, and also because he saw
> the rest of the Greek world taking one side or the other, some
> right away, others planning to do so. This was certainly the
> greatest upheaval there had ever been among the Greeks. It
> also reached many foreigners – indeed, one might say that it
> affected most people everywhere. (I.1)

The Peloponnesian War lasted from 431 to 404 B.C., and even
though Thucydides survived the war, his account stops in
411, with seven years of the war left unwritten.

As for the earlier wars, Thucydides was thinking of the
Trojan War (c. 1200) about which Homer (c. 750) had sung,
and the Persian War (499–479) about which Herodotus
(c. 484–425) – the father of history according to Cicero – had
written. Homer's *Iliad* is an epic poem, a story of heroes
and of the war between the Greeks and the Trojans. An
epic is also concerned with greatness and what is worthy
of being remembered, but it is not history. Herodotus and
Thucydides knew that the Trojan War had occurred, but
they also knew that they were doing something different
from Homer. A poet may invent and exaggerate; a historian
may not.

Figure 1. The Greek hero Odysseus cuts the throat of a Thracian soldier, c. 540 B.C. After a scene from the *Iliad*. The Thracians were allies of the Trojans.

Several sections later in his book, Thucydides returns to the comment with which he began:

> People always think the greatest war is the one they are fighting at the moment, and when that is over they are more impressed with wars of antiquity; but, even so, this war will prove, to all who look at the facts, that it was greater than the others. (1.21)

Once again, Thucydides emphasizes that the Peloponnesian War was the greatest of all wars. He is not concerned with the glory (*kleos*) that individuals attained during the war with their actions – even though the name of the muse of history, Clio (*Kleiô*), is etymologically related to glory. Thucydides is concerned with the numerous war efforts and the magnitude of suffering it caused and how that makes the war 'worthy of note' (*axiologon*). This is what 'greatness' means to him.

> The greatest action before this was the one against the Persians, and even that was decided quickly by two battles at sea and two on land. But the Peloponnesian war went on for a very long time and brought more suffering to Greece than had ever been seen before: never had so many cities been captured and depopulated (some by foreigners, others by Greeks themselves at war with one another – some of which were resettled with new inhabitants); never had so many people been driven from their countries or killed, either in the war itself or as a result of civil strife. (1.23)

This once more makes it clear how Thucydides' history differs from the epic tradition. In the Homeric poems, the glorious deeds of heroes take centre stage, not the magnitude of the war and the suffering it caused.

Elements of our concept of history can be found in the works of the first historians. There are also differences between these ancient and modern conceptions of history. These, too, will be addressed in this chapter.

There were historians before Herodotus and Thucydides, the so-called logographers, who wrote histories of peoples, cities, and noble houses; in these histories, the logographers were also attentive to the geographical and ethnographical particularities. Only a single fragment of their work is preserved. Herodotus was the first to use the word *historiê* – variously translated as 'research' or 'inquiry' – to describe his work.

But Thucydides, who does not use that word, became the model for the historian whose aim it is to say what has been done, as Lucian (c. 120–190) put it. When Thucydides' work was rediscovered in the fifteenth century, and later, when history became an academic discipline in the nineteenth century, he became *the* model for the historian. Thucydides is the first true historian, and the most perfect historian to have ever lived, Niebuhr tells us, dubbing Thucydides the Homer among the historians. Leopold von Ranke (1795–1886), who devoted his doctoral dissertation to Thucydides and is himself often called the father of modern history-writing, agrees with this judgement. His claim that the task of the historian is to say what the past was really like, *wie es eigentlich gewesen*, is said to have been drawn from Thucydides.

The war broke out when Athens was at the height of its power and influence. Thucydides focuses his history on the political aspects giving rise to the conflict between Athens and Sparta and their consequences. The representation of the suffering and the insight he offers into human nature still impresses the reader. He is concerned with power, empire, justice, violence, disasters, fear, honour, and human self-interest; the contrast between what people expect, hope, and want; and the actual course of the events. Thucydides was himself dismissed as a general and exiled for 20 years after he failed to keep the Athenian colony Amphipolis out of Spartan hands in the winter of 424. It gave him, he writes, the needed time to study the war closely.

Fact and Fiction

In the introduction to his work, Thucydides complains that not only the poets but also historians, too, are in the habit of giving exaggerated, embellished accounts of what has happened. In a famous methodological passage – the first systematic exposition of historical criticism – he criticizes both poets and historians:

> But if the evidence cited leads a reader to think that things were mostly as I have described them, he would not go wrong, as he would if he believed what the poets have sung about them, which they have much embellished, or what the historians [*logographoi*] have strung together, which aims more to delight the ear than to be true. Their accounts cannot be tested, you see, and many are not credible, as they have achieved the status of myth over time. (I.21)

Thucydides wants to narrate the events as they actually happened.

> I did not think it right to set down either what I heard from people I happened to meet or what I merely believed to be true. Even for events at which I was present myself, I tracked down detailed information from other sources as far as I could. (I.22)

The description of what has been done – the facts, we would say – depends on what the historian himself is able to observe and ascertain, and on the critical examination of eyewitness reports. Evidence that supports his account need to be assessed with accuracy (*akribeia*). Embellishment and unconfirmed claims have no place in a true history. Herodotus, who is most likely also criticized in this passage, though he is not named, also distinguished between what he was able to see for himself and what he heard from others. He, however, chose to write down and include what others said: not because he believed it to be true, but simply because it was reported. It would do his reputation no good.

The emphasis on *autopsy* ('seeing for oneself') characterizes the *histor* ('knower'). Herodotus and Thucydides thus join what would become a long line of scholars and scientists who consider empirical observation – seeing for oneself – as the foundation of science. Not that knowledge of what has been done is limited to a sensory impression: Both Herodotus and Thucydides knew that the eyes may deceive and that reports are often biased. Thucydides writes:

> It was hard work to find out what happened, because those who were present at each event gave different reports, depending on which side they favoured and how well they remembered. (I.22)

The bias of eyewitnesses and the selectivity of memory are obstacles the historian needs to overcome. Thucydides also observes that eyewitnesses often see no more than what happens in their immediate environment. For these reasons it is important for historians to compare multiple accounts with one another. The critical study of eyewitness reports and other primary sources has remained foundational for historical studies to this day. The historian establishes facts and neither invents nor embellishes. Thucydides mainly relies on what he himself was able to observe and on the critical examination of what others have seen and heard. He writes a contemporary history. But for the early history which he discusses in the introductory sections of his work, he depends primarily on oral traditions. The exception is the one archaeological find he mentions. Elsewhere in his book he uses local annals (chronological overviews of events year by year) and treaties.

Political History

Thucydides not only represents the course of events of the war but also aims to explain how the Athenians and Spartans found themselves at war with each other. In this he emulates Herodotus, who had started his history by asking how the enmity between the Greeks and Persians had arisen. Explaining events is an important element of any historical study and an element that we still associate with history as a discipline today. Herodotus is interested in the question of guilt and the person who committed the first unlawful act that caused the enmity between the Persians and Greeks. At the end of his own methodological passage, however, Thucydides offers a different kind of explanation, which does not ascribe the war to the single act of any individual:

> I believe that the truest reason for the quarrel, though least evident in what was said at the time, was the growth of Athenian power, which put fear into the Spartans and so compelled them into war. (I.23)

The growth of Athenian power and the fear it induced is what caused the war and perhaps made it inevitable, at least in the eyes of the principal actors on both sides. The Athenians had no choice but to maintain their empire. The Spartans were rightfully alarmed by it. This explanation is typical of the political history that Thucydides wrote. A certain situation compels one to act in a certain way, even if it might have been wiser to act differently.

Thucydides' analysis of the war is to a large extent presented in the speeches given by the various parties involved. These speeches make up almost a quarter of his work. Many took place in public. All are stylistically and argumentatively polished. Here is what he has to say about them:

> What particular people said in their speeches, either just before or during the war, was hard to recall exactly, whether they were speeches I heard myself or those that were reported to me at second hand. I have made each speaker say what I thought his situation demanded, keeping as near as possible to the general sense of what was actually said. (I.22)

The speeches enable Thucydides to present the points of view of the main actors in the war and their motives. These speeches provide him with a means to demonstrate his impartiality. Here, impartiality entails the recognition that, from the point of view of others, differing interests, beliefs, and desires should be deemed important. The speeches also tie his narrative to the world in which he lived and (on the Athenian side) to the idea of citizenship in a democratic polis, where in a debate one had to exchange one's own opinion for a moment for that of one's opponent in order to understand how he had arrived at his views. The speeches also link Thucydides' account to Sophism, the dominant philosophy in Athens and its sister cities at that time, which emphasized that both positions in a dispute need to be discussed and substantiated.

As a resident of the Athenian polis, Thucydides is interested in political life, which is the domain of the free man and citizen, and from which women, foreigners, and slaves were excluded. His history is thus a *political* history. He is concerned with power, justice, war, treaties, negotiations, military actions, leadership, and the functioning of political institutions. Even a dramatic event such as the plague in Athens in the summer of 430, shortly after the onset of war, is described in terms of its political consequences – Thucydides emphasizes how it led to the social disintegration of the city. His close attention to the fortunes of the city, its politics, and the sufferings caused by the war, stand in sharp contrast with the work of the good-humoured cosmopolitan Herodotus. As a traveller, he had set out to record the ethnographic and geographical particularities of the regions he visited, as had his predecessors, the logographers. Only at a later stage did he conceive his plan to write the history of the Persian wars.

The view that history is primarily political history would remain influential for a long time. Not only in antiquity but also well into the 20th century this view would dominate, despite Herodotus's work and his attention to the ethnographic and geographical particularities of the peoples and places he visited during his travels. If later historians paid attention to these particularities, it would be as part of the political history they wrote.

Modern historians do not include speeches in their work. But the idea behind the speeches has always remained part of history-writing. Placing oneself into the perspective of another person is part of the work of the historian who wants to understand the motives and thoughts of people in the past. This will be further discussed in Chapter 4. The modern historian also knows that differences in points of view stem from differences in interests, beliefs, and desires.

Figure 2. Greek soldier attacks Persian soldier, c. 480–470. Usually the war scenes depicted on terracotta are based on Greek myths.

Realism: The Melian Dialogue

Thucydides allows his readers to follow the course of the war closely and alternates his account between winters and summers. This was innovative compared to those historians who had used annals as their chronological framework. It suits the history he writes wherein military actions are related to seasons – summer and winter being the two traditional campaigning periods. A well-known episode in his work is the Melian dialogue, which occurred during the summer of 416 B.C. It provides a good reflection of his conception of history.

During this season, in the midst of a brief suspension of hostilities with Sparta, the Athenians dispatched an expedition to the island of Melos, a colony originally founded by the Spartans. Melos had not, unlike the other islands, submitted to the Athenians, who were lords and masters of the sea, but had chosen to remain neutral. The negotiation that the Melians initiated with the Athenian expedition army is indicative of Thucydides' view of war, history, and the nature of man. A number of things stand out in the negotiations, which incidentally were not held in public (the Athenians suspect that the Melian leadership did not dare to negotiate in the open).

The first thing that strikes us is that the Melians, at crucial moments in the negotiations, emphasize their future expectations, while the Athenians constantly place priority on the here and now, the factuality of the moment. A second noticeable point is that, due to the inequality of the balance of power between the Athenians and the Melians, justice cannot be upheld. In such cases, might supersedes right. The Athenians state the following:

> Let's work out what we can do on the basis of what both sides truly accept: we both know that decisions about justice are made in human discussions only when both sides are under equal compulsion; but when one side is stronger, it gets as much as it can, and the weak must accept that. (v.89)

The Melians respond that they want to stay neutral and do not want to choose sides. But the Athenians note that the friendship the Melians offer is worse than their enmity: If they were to accept it, it would be evidence of Athenian weakness, while their enmity will provide evidence of Athenian power. The Athenians emphasize that it is not a negotiation between equals. The Melians in turn say that they do not want to give up hope. Unlike the Athenians, they put the future first. Hope only brings comfort in times of danger, the Athenians say. The Melians respond, again based on a certain future expectation, by saying the following:

> We trust that our good fortune will be no less than yours. The gods are on our side, because we stand innocent against men who are unjust. And as for power, what we lack will be supplied by the alliance we will make with the Spartans, who must defend us as a matter of honour, if only because we are related to them. So our confidence is not as totally unreasonable as you might think. (v.104)

The Athenians are not impressed by these arguments. They, too, have no reason to doubt the good will of the gods, for the Athenians do nothing contrary to the beliefs of the gods of man:

> Well, the favour of the gods should be as much on our side as yours. Neither our principles nor our actions are contrary to what men believe about the gods, or would want for them-selves. Nature always compels gods (we believe) and men (we are certain) to rule over anyone they can control. We did not make this law, and we were not the first to follow it; but we will take it as we found it and leave it to posterity forever, because we know that you would do the same if you had our power, and so would anyone else. So as far as the favour of the gods is concerned, we have no reason to fear that we will do worse than you. (v.105)

The Athenians are left with no other option than to exert their power. They are not unjust in doing so, because justice comes from power, as was taught by the sophists, who strongly influenced Thucydides. As for the hope of support from the Spartans, the Athenians wish the Melians luck: They do not expect it to arrive. The Athenians conclude:

> Your strongest points are mere hopes for the future, and your actual resources are too small for your survival in view of the forces arrayed against you. (v.111)

The choice for the Melians is a binary one: either war with Athens or submission to their rule. The Melians do not want to give up their freedom. As the Athenians observe, they are the only ones who have a clearer picture of the future than of the here and now. While the present is for everyone to see, the Melians only consider the future to which they aspire as real.

The outcome of the negotiations is that the Athenians besiege the city. The Melians finally surrender, after betrayal among their own. The result is reported without further comment or judgement:

> The Athenians killed all the men of military age and made slaves of the women and children. Later, they settled the place themselves, sending five hundred colonists. (v.116)

This kind of factual description, and the harsh reality of war that emerges, characterizes the work of Thucydides. Thucydides relates the negotiations from a specific point of view. The Athenians are realists, as they focus on the moment and on their strength, while the Melians rest their hopes on a future reversal of fortune and on the will of the gods, trusting that justice will prevail.

This is not to say that Thucydides simply accepts reality as it is. He constantly warns his readers that war is a violent teacher, and stresses how easily man gives in to doing what he does not really want to do, driven by fear, self-interest, and honour. Society easily disintegrates when it is struck by a disaster such as the plague in Athens, or as a consequence of civil strife, such as occured in the city of Corcyra in 427, when all things civil instantly crumbled and man's brutal nature surfaced. Thucydides strongly laments such courses of events. He doesn't do so in case of the fate of the Melians and simply describes what happened to them because he sees the Melians as responsible for their own fate, blind to the realities of their situation.

It is this strict, honest, and often harsh realism that would make such an impression on Nietzsche and why, in his own words, he felt most closely related to Thucydides, in whom he saw a typical old Hellene (Hellas is the native name of Greece). The Athenian's history of the Peloponnesian War contains no embellishment but only the strict factuality of the moment. There is no underlying idea or principle that steers the course of events and justifies a hopeful future. This does not mean, however, that his history has no message, as we will see.

The Melian dialogue brings to the fore an important general insight into history-writing: A historian's specific point of view, and the political and moral standards that characterize it, are what make a certain kind of history-writing possible. Think of the realism in Thucydides' description of interstate politics, the emphasis on looking at both sides in a dispute, and the sophists' view that, especially in times of war, might will supersede right. Such political and moral standards determine the historian's focus in his work and how he assesses that which has been done.

The Value of History

Thucydides tells us that he intends for his history to be a possession for all times. Its message is clear: It is in the nature of man to pursue honour and self-interest, and he is often guided by fear. Societies easily disintegrate when confronted with disasters and other setbacks. There is also the cruel reality that in the relationships between states, whenever there is a need to invoke questions of 'right', justice inevitably derives from power. Might makes right, as the saying goes. But human beings are also capable of not falling back on their most basic human nature (*anthropeia phusis*). The moral order can be upheld by men of reason:

> In peace and prosperity, cities and private individuals alike are better minded because they are not plunged into the necessity of doing anything against their will; but war is a violent teacher: it gives most people impulses that are as bad as their situation when it takes away the easy supply of what they need for daily life. (III.82)

This is the lesson that Thucydides wants his audience to learn and the reason why his historical work has, in fact, become a possession for all times. In times of peace and prosperity, man is at his best, and able to put justice and the general interest first. But in times of war many lose sight of that, and honour, fear, and self-interest take over. Such is the nature of man. It ensures that the course of events will exhibit a certain necessity (*ananke*) in that his nature compels man to behave in a certain way in particular circumstances, and it is against this that Thucydides warns us.

Previously I stated that the answers to what history is and why it is useful are mutually dependent. This also becomes apparent in the work of Thucydides. He states:

> Those who want to look into the truth of what was done in the past – which, given the human condition, will recur in the future, either in same fashion or nearly so – those readers will find this work valuable enough, as this was composed to be a lasting possession and not to be heard for a prize at the moment of a contest. (I.22)

History offers insights into man's nature and, with it, thoughts as to how the future may unfold. Thucydides does not actually claim to be able to predict the future, or to know the direction of history and how events will proceed. But he does claim to know human nature and how, as long as it remains essentially the same, it will lead to certain behaviour in certain circumstances. This is what makes history useful. For this reason, Thucydides focuses on human nature when he explains why events in the Peloponnesian War happened as they did.

Thucydides has a pessimistic message for his readers. People are naturally inclined to be guided by honour, fear, and self-interest. In times of peace and prosperity it is possible to pursue higher ideals and to be guided by reason, but in case of setbacks people are inclined to do things that in other circumstances they would not wish to do. A few people realize this and are able, even when their reason is tested, to evade this impulse from human nature. Such a person was the Athenian leader Pericles (c. 495–429), to whose circle Thucydides belonged. After Pericles' death as a result of the plague, Athens did not survive. The Athenians lost the war because, after Pericles' death, the city's new leaders pursued their self-interest and told the people what they wanted to hear instead of what would be the right course of action in the general interests of the city. Democracy itself was unable to withstand the war. Athens was at its prime when the war broke out, but its power proved transient because of the actions of its own population and as a result of human nature. Such was the tragic fate of Athens.

Thucydides' depiction of the plague and the disastrous expedition against Sicily, which would signal the beginning of the end for the Athenians, still makes a great impression on the reader. The work's realism centres on injustice, suffering, the uncertainty of what happens, and a human nature that shows how man is unable to control the situation in which he finds himself. The lessons from Thucydides are not practical – he does not give direct advice on what to do in specific circumstances. This is not the purpose of his work. Rather, it offers a view of human nature, while at the same time confirming the temporality and uncertainty of human existence, and the importance of having the reality of the moment in view. This should be, according to Thucydides, the focus of history-writing.

Mortality and Eternity

In the opening passage of his work, Herodotus writes that history is concerned with what comes into being because of man (*ta genomena ex anthrôpôn*), with what man has done and created. Herodotus thus separates the human from the natural. The human is what man brings forth. The natural comes into being by itself. (Note that the Greek gods did not create the world: They had to conquer it.) Men are mortal and only exist once. Nature is immortal because it keeps returning. The fact that Herodotus also pays attention to different explanations of natural phenomena, such as the annual flooding of the Nile, means that his work, apart from being a history, is also a treatise on geography.

The distinction between the mortality of man and the eternity of nature, between what exists because of man and what exists in itself, between what exists in time only once and what forever returns, makes it clear what belongs to the domain of history. The distinction between our man-made world and that of nature will be made time and again in later centuries. The philosopher Hannah Arendt (1906–1975), while discussing the relation between the modern and the ancient concept of history, writes the following about it in her essay, 'The Modern Concept of History':

> These single instances, deeds or events, interrupt the circular movement of daily life in the same sense that the rectilinear *bios* of the mortals interrupts the circular movement of biological life [*zoe*]. The subject matter of history is these interruptions, the extraordinary, in other words. (p. 572)

To the extent that man is a natural being, he is immortal; as a species he always returns, just like any other part of nature. Mortality is what characterizes temporary, individual life, which only takes place once in time: linearly, from birth to death. It is therefore at odds with the cyclical and eternally recurring nature of biological life. However, that eternity is not entirely beyond the reach of man. Memory is able to endow man with immortality: Mnemosyne, the goddess of memory, is the mother of all muses for good reason. Herodotus calls upon her in the opening passage of his work: He wants to protect what has been done from fading into oblivion. Thucydides begins his work with the observation that the war between Athens and Sparta is greater and more memorable than all the previous ones, and therefore it must be recorded.

A historian provides a specific answer to the question of what is memorable and therefore what deserves to be immortal. It is a different answer than that given by the epic poets. It also differs from what the Greek philosophers would say in attempting to get a grip on what is great and memorable in their own fashion. For Plato (c. 427–347) and his student Aristotle (384–322), immortality only comes within the reach of man when he manages to be in the vicinity of eternal things. Man is not denied the possibility of attaining immortality, Arendt notes, but he is denied the possibility

> of measuring himself and his own deeds against the everlasting greatness of the cosmos, to match, as it were, the immortality of nature and the gods with an immortal greatness of his own. (pp. 575–576)

Plato and Aristotle were of the opinion that the deeds of man could not have a significance that transcends their temporal existence. Their view leaves no room for the historian who seeks to immortalize that which was great and memorable.

In her own essay, Arendt makes no mention of Nietzsche and his conception of history, which we discussed in the previous chapter. But she must have had him in mind. Nietzsche would return to the ancient 'pre-Socratic' Greeks (those that precede Plato), of whom he considered himself a student, and argue that only the truly great things of the past are worthy of being known and preserved. For him, too, the great deeds of the past are everlasting. Nietzsche thus preferred the historian's answer to the question of what deserves immortality above the response of the philosopher.

With regard to the greatness of man and his deeds, Nietzsche particularly had in mind the geniuses of the past and their works. The history of Thucydides is such a great and timeless work. It allows us to look at the world in a different way, which gives it strength and value. With regard to greatness, Thucydides himself reflected on the extent of the war and the suffering caused by it, both of which made it greater than all previous wars. Nietzsche has little to say about this sense of greatness in the essay we discussed in the previous chapter. He does however address it elsewhere in his work, as we will see in Chapter 7 of this book.

I conclude this chapter by noting some important differences between the ancient and modern understandings of history.

Single Instances and Processes

Thucydides recorded the Peloponnesian War in the expectation that it would be a major conflict. It is crucial to note that the memorable deeds and events that Herodotus, Thucydides, and other Greek historians wrote about were not linked to the idea that history itself has a meaning, direction, or purpose: A conception of history which, for example, characterizes Hebrew thought and which later would enter Christian theology, in which religion and history are intertwined. Nor do the memorable events of which the first historians wrote contribute to some development or process, such as the growth of the nation or the emergence of an empire – something we come across for the first time in the historiography of Rome. What is great and memorable according to the ancient Greeks is great and memorable in and of itself, whether it be the glorious acts of the heroes on the battlefield in Homer's epic, the memorable deeds of individuals in the history of Herodotus, or, on a larger scale, the very magnitude of the Peloponnesian War and the suffering it caused – as is the case in the work of Thucydides.

Arendt has the following to say about this early concept of history:

> What is difficult for us to realize is that the great deeds and works of which mortals are capable, and which become the topic of historical narrative, are not seen as parts either of an encompassing whole or a process; on the contrary, the stress is always on single instances and single gestures. (p. 572)

Now we can understand Nietzsche's comment quoted in the previous chapter. According to him, the best specimens of man on whom historical studies should focus were not deemed to be continuing some kind of process. Their works are great in themselves and not merely the products of the context in which they were created or the causes of developments to which they contributed. Nietzsche thereby turned against the academic perspective on history prevalent in his own time and returned to the view of the ancient Greeks.

Arendt continues with the observation that only in late antiquity did people start to think of history in terms of *processes*.

> When in late antiquity speculations began about the nature of history in the sense of a historical process and about the historical fate of nations, their rise and fall, where the particular actions and events were engulfed in a whole, it was at once assumed that these processes must be circular. The historical movement began to be construed in the image of biological life. (p. 572)

As a consequence of this shift, the idea that mortals were to acquire immortality through their deeds was lost.

It is not clear what Arendt has in mind when she writes that processes must be circular. There were, in late antiquity, theorists who speculated about the renewal of worlds, and thus posited the view of the renewal of history. We also know of Greek and Roman theories on the succession of governments (Polybius, following Aristotle, posits a famous version of this idea); these theories propose that the succession of governments eventually ends up with the type of government with which it began, initiating a further succession of governments. And certain philosophies such as Stoicism theorized a cycle of successive universes. But there were no *historians* in antiquity who held a cyclical view of time itself. I mention this because sometimes the Christian church father Augustine of Hippo (354–430) is credited with being the first philosopher of history and for having influenced the modern conception of time because of his criticism of the theorists speculating about cyclical time and the renewals of worlds in his *De Civitate Dei* (*City of God*). The idea of the renewal of worlds was obviously opposed to the Christian view of the unique and linear history of mankind, starting with God's creation, which includes the creation of time itself, and ending with his final judgement at the end of time. Augustine, however, was not interested in the historical significance of secular events. As Arendt writes:

> The fall of Rome, occurring in his lifetime, was interpreted by Christians and pagans alike as a decisive event, and it was to the refutation of this belief that Augustine devoted thirteen years of his life [to write his *De Civitate Dei*]. The point, as he saw it, was that no purely secular event could or should ever be of central import to man. (p. 66)

It is therefore not Augustine's understanding of history on which the modern concept of history rests. Rather, it is the combination of the idea of events contributing to some type of forward development with the concept of the polity as a political-moral unity that is central to the modern concept of history. Both ideas were absent in the work of Greek historians. They simply could not include individual deeds in some kind of developmental process because they did not contribute to any kind of entity exhibiting political-moral unity.

The idea of national history is a modern one, but can be found in a prototypical form among the Romans and was carried over to modern times through the work of Renaissance humanists. The historians writing about Roman history did so from the perspective of Rome as a polity or political body. The Romans did not use the term 'nation' for this: There was no *natio Romanorum*, but there was a *populus Romanus* (the term 'nation' was used to designate a community of foreigners of the same origin). Nevertheless, for the sake of simplicity, I shall use the term 'national history' to refer to any history conveying the origins and development of an integrated political entity. The first who wrote such a work, and to whom we owe the origins of national history, is Quintus Fabius Pictor (254–201). Between 215 and his death, Pictor wrote a history of Rome from its foundation until the second Punic War between Carthage and Rome. This work is now lost but known in parts through references to it in the works of later writers. Its emphasis on political institutions and their continuity, and the idea of a nation, contributed a new and, in retrospect, critical component to our understanding of history. When history became an academic discipline in the nineteenth century, the nation

– by that point, rapidly transitioning into the modern nation-state – provided the natural framework for the histories being written.

The idea that historical developments were presented in the image of biological life, as Arendt observes, also points to something else. Nineteenth-century historians such as Niebuhr and Ranke, as well as philosophers such as Georg Wilhelm Friedrich Hegel (1770–1831), were influenced by romantic thinkers such as Johann Gottfried Herder (1744–1803) who, in their response to the Enlightenment and its somewhat mechanical world view, returned to an older, more organic conception of nature which they applied to their understanding of the nation. Every nation has its own character and leads its own life. Every nation exists in and for itself, as Hegel would have it. What people do and what they bring forth expresses the specific character of that nation, thus contributing to its realization. In the nineteenth century, scholars started to think in a new way about the past and the historical process, in which the rise and greatness of nations became central.

History Coming to a Close

In contrast to Herodotus and Thucydides, who focused predominantly on their own time, the fourth-century Greek historian Ephorus of Cuma (c. 400–330), who lived a generation after Thucydides and whose work is as good as lost, focused on the (distant) past and was the first to write a continuous history of the Greeks from around 1200 B.C. up to his own time. When Niebuhr, in his *Vorträge über alte Geschichte* (*Lectures on Ancient History*), explains why these historians' approaches differed, he does so in a typical romantic, nineteenth-century manner:

> It is in the nature of things that the Greeks at that time [the fourth century B.C.] diligently went over their ancient history, whereas they had previously ignored it or had been indifferent to it; but they could no longer deny that their history had come to a close, that the rising star of Macedonian greatness eclipsed the star of Athens and Greece, and that Greek history in its prime was coming to an end. (p. 209)

In Herodotus's time, it was felt that everything was moving forwards, but they still focused on the flourishing present rather than on the past. It did not occur to the Greeks, Niebuhr tells us, to 'close the totality of Greek history and treat it as a whole'. Only with the end in sight, when the 'evening over Greece dawned', did such a treatment become possible.

These passages are characteristic of the romantic sense of the past at the beginning of the nineteenth century. This is evident from the vocabulary derived from nature when speaking about history: the rising star, the flourishing of a nation, the evening that dawns. History is understood in the image of biological life. This is also apparent from the idea that a form of life may grow old, as Hegel would have it, and come to a close. The coming to an end, and the sense of loss associated with it, is an impulse for historical awareness, and makes one focus on the past, for one wants to know what one has lost. For Hegel, there is only history when there are developments, revolutions, and endings, when something changes and we become aware of the transience of empires and peoples – that is why he calls the Persians the first historical people, because their empire was the first to perish.

The difference between Herodotus and Thucydides on the one hand and Ephorus on the other is that Herodotus and Thucydides shared the 'spirit' of what they described, while Ephorus tried to understand the entire history of the Greeks from his own mind. Hegel therefore calls the contemporary histories of Herodotus and Thucydides, which he knew well and admired, and also, for example, the history of the Renaissance historian Francesco Guicciardini (1483–1540), *original* histories. He names histories such as those of Ephorus and Niebuhr, in which one's own time is transcended and one looks back on forms of life that are gone, *reflective* histories.

There are many differences between the first Greek historians and the earliest modern historians such as Niebuhr and Ranke, some of which have been discussed in this chapter. The concept of history at the beginning of the nineteenth century is the subject of the next chapter, which aims to shed more light on what, exactly, was new in the modern concept of history.

3. Historicism

Niebuhr was the first professor of history at the newly founded University of Berlin in 1810. There, a separate faculty for history was created, permitting history to become an independent academic discipline, with its own standards and rules, and, in their wake, its own academic journals, research institutes, and organizations. Until then, history had been taught as a sub-discipline of law or theology, and was understood mainly as philosophy teaching by example: The past offered examples from which general political and moral principles could be drawn. Before history became an academic discipline, the study of the past was the domain of politicians, diplomats, and other civil servants. Niebuhr himself was not a historian by profession. Prior to his appointment, he was, among other things, secretary of the Danish finance minister, director of the national bank of Denmark, and an employee of the Prussian government. In 1815, he would become the Prussian ambassador to the Vatican.

Every Wednesday and Saturday morning during the winter semester at Berlin, Niebuhr lectured on the history of Rome from 10 to 11. His lectures attracted a large audience of not only students and colleagues, but also officers and others interested in his work. They were, if we are to believe his colleague and professor of law Friedrich Carl von Savigny (1779–1861), 'the fairest harbinger of the future eminence of the youthful university'. Niebuhr did something new: He took a critical stance towards Roman history-writing, separated its facts from its fabrications, and he went in search of the *ethos* – the moral character – of the Romans as it was reflected in their customs, habits, laws, and institutions. With it, Savigny said, Niebuhr opened 'a new era for Roman history'.

Ranke became a professor at the University of Berlin in 1825. By then, Niebuhr was lecturing at the university of Bonn. Ranke is often regarded as the father of modern history-writing. He studied Niebuhr's work closely and saw himself as his student: At least, that's what he wrote in 1824 in a letter accompanying a copy of his first book which he sent to Niebuhr. Later in his life, Ranke would point out that Niebuhr's work was a textbook example of historical research. Niebuhr himself stated that the discipline of history first came to fruition in his generation. He put the unity of education and research into practice, exactly as the founder of the University of Berlin, the linguist Wilhelm von Humboldt (1767–1835), had envisioned. In one of his letters, Niebuhr praised Ranke's history of Serbia and his handling of its sources, expecting the younger scholar to remain an excellent historian and writer.

The influence of Niebuhr and especially Ranke on history as an academic discipline would be large. They not only had specific views on how the discipline should be practised but also on history itself as a process. Their view of history is known as historicism. Developed further by many other historians and philosophers throughout the nineteenth century, it is the central subject of this chapter.

Historicism is the view that history is a science which studies what is specific (*eigen*) to the development *in* time of individual communities – nations – and their ethos, and their contribution to the development of mankind as a whole. The term 'historicism' was not initially used to describe this view, and it was not until around 1900 that it came to be closely associated with history as an academic discipline and the ideas of history on which it was based.

Central to the historicists' understanding of the past was the state, which, to them, was the embodiment of the moral character of the nation as an organic whole. This organic conception of communities was not something new, as we noted in the previous chapter. But the notion that every nation has its centre in itself, as Herder wrote, and is a spiritual individuality (*Geistiger Individualität*), as Humboldt called it, was new. In his lectures on the philosophy of history in the 1820s, Hegel said that the entities (*Individuen*) that we encounter in world history are nations (*Völker*). He called those nations 'states' in the same breath. The romantic view of the nation is found among all historicists at the start of the nineteenth century; in Niebuhr, Humboldt, Ranke, and (from a different, philosophical perspective) Hegel. Decisive for their ideas about the historical process was the French Revolution.

The French Revolution and Historical Awareness

The importance of the French Revolution for the new, modern concept of history in the nineteenth century has often been emphasized. Niebuhr's, Humboldt's, Hegel's, and Ranke's work would not have taken the forms they did had the Revolution not occurred. The Revolution was also decisive in a practical sense. The University of Berlin, where these scholars lectured and where history became an academic discipline, was founded as part of the efforts to 'renew' Prussia after the Prussian army had suffered a devastating defeat at the hands of Napoleon's French troops in Jena and Auerstedt in 1806.

The Revolution and its Napoleonic aftermath made a deep impression on its contemporaries, not only because of the changes it brought about in the sociopolitical order in France and the countries it waged war against, but also because of the atrocities, terror, and devastation of the revolutionary and Napoleonic wars, and the disruption and uncertainty which accompanied these events.

To Niebuhr, the French Revolution made it clear that it was vital to study the past. This is what he says about it in his *Vortrage über römische Alterthümer* (*Lectures on Roman Antiquity*):

> As a child I saw the atrocities with horror, I saw that the old constitution was different from the new one, and how there was a lack of knowledge of antiquity in the many things that were said about it. (p. 6)

Niebuhr was twelve years old when the Bastille was stormed in July 1789, an event which would mark the beginning of the Revolution. But his memory of the events made him realize that the past was essentially different from the present, and that knowledge of the past was needed to interpret the rupture brought about by the Revolution. In his letters, we find similar views – about the horrors of the Revolution and the disruption of the familiar world. An age was coming to an end. In May 1809, he wrote:

> I am constantly asking myself here, whether we are really living in the same age of the world that we did formerly, when we calmly reckoned beforehand on the future, or built castles in the air; or whether all before us is not, as it seems to our eyes, Chaos and Night – a universal destruction of all that now exists? (pp. 193–194)

During the Revolution and the Napoleonic age, events followed upon one another at a rapid pace. It seemed as if time itself had accelerated. At least that's how it was experienced by many. Such experiences contributed to the widely shared feeling that a new age had begun. Fittingly, the time before the Revolution came to be known as the *ancien régime*, the old regime. It was also the aim of the revolutionaries to bring about something new and thus end the sociopolitical order they knew. Their intention was not simply to restore a previous situation that had been corrupted, as, for instance, had been the case in England's Glorious Revolution of 1688.

In April 1814, after the first abdication of Napoleon, Niebuhr congratulated Europe 'on the establishment of civil liberty on a practicable and durable basis'. He wrote enthusiastically:

> A remarkable age is still before us; the world will not sink back into its old insipidity and sluggishness again for the rest of our lifetime, and the foundation may be laid for better times. (p. 277)

The world would eventually, he hoped, change for the better. It would be futile, Niebuhr believed, to try to restore what was lost. The progression of history could not be undone by being reversed. This same attitude towards the politics of restoration is found in Hegel.

It has been argued that Hegel's philosophy *is* a philosophy of revolution. Every year, he would celebrate the anniversary of the storming of the Bastille. The French Revolution was, to him, a world-historical event, despite its terror and the devastation it caused. And after seeing him enter Jena in 1806, he called Napoleon a *Weltseele* ('world soul') on horseback; a man who had set the history of the world in motion.

Napoleon's actions made it clear that one person could be the embodiment of major historical changes in the world.

Hegel concludes his *Vorlesungen über die Philosophie der Geschichte* (*Lectures on the Philosophy of History*) with the effects that the French victories had on Germany. First, he observes that it had banished the idea of a German empire (in the sense that one had existed throughout the Middle Ages and subsequent centuries) completely and replaced it with sovereign states. Most important to Hegel, however, was the new law system which was the result of the French oppression:

> Feudal relations are abolished, the principles of freedom of property and of person are made into founding principles. Every citizen has access to civil offices, for which skill and usefulness are necessary conditions. Government rests on the world of civil servants. (p. 604)

The monarch was still sovereign, but his decisions were not arbitrary; rather, they were drawn from within the boundaries set by the organization of the state and its laws.

Freedom, the Revolution had proclaimed, was an inalienable right for all. This is why Hegel believed that the Revolution had universal significance and value. It was the fulfilment of the promise of the old Germanic ideal of civil freedom and equality – the latter being a widely spread conception which, for instance, was also held by Niebuhr, according to one of his letters written in 1818. Like Niebuhr, Hegel believed that the Revolution had to be understood historically, and like Niebuhr, Hegel thought that there was no possible return to the situation that had existed before the Revolution, despite the restoration politics of his day. Philosophical history was to make the Revolution intelligible, which meant to Hegel that the development of human social-mindedness (*Geist*), and how it had eventually resulted in the Revolution, needed to be studied.

We should note that Hegel, in company with the other historicists, was a child of his time (to use his own words) so far as gender was concerned: The public sphere of the state and its freedom were reserved for men, not for women. We should also note that the universal significance of the French Revolution, and more generally, of European developments, betray a Eurocentric view of the world. Hegel does discuss the oriental world and Africa – the latter with overly condescending and racist overtones and the former as a world at a standstill, surpassed by Europe ever since the Greeks. But he has little to say about developments in the world outside of Europe in his own day. He considers slavery a great injustice which should be abolished; he discusses this in, among others, his *Vorlesungen* and his 1821 *Philosophie des Rechts* (*Philosophy of Right*). Colonialism, however, is discussed only briefly (in his *Philosophie des Rechts*) as part of international trade and how trade has world-historical significance because it brings with it legal contracts and judicial relations. To become part of history, Hegel asserts, events have to occur within a framework of legislation that only the state can provide. He, however, turned a blind eye to how European states were obstacles to freedom and justice elsewhere in the world. Just like his fellow historicists, Hegel was incapable of seeing how developments outside of Europe could be significant and of value in themselves, independent from European developments and conceptions thereof.

Hegel's philosophy is, as we said, a philosophy of revolution – and not only of the French Revolution, but also of the Haitian Revolution (1791–1804). Hegel's many remarks on slavery were in part made in response to this revolution and the independent state that the self-liberated slaves established in Haiti. This revolution, too, had world-historical significance. Hegel's philosophy of revolution is a philosophy of the realization of freedom. Man, as man, is free. Both the French Revolution and its Haitian counterpart had turned this idea into a social and political reality.

The Historical School

Central to history as an academic discipline is the critical attitude towards documentary evidence. The historian must discern the way in which truth has enveloped itself in the sources, Niebuhr wrote. The existing knowledge of the history of Rome, he believed, was mistaken and imperfect. He came to this conclusion after his studies during his leisure time while still in the civil service. In one of his letters in May 1804 he wrote:

> I was straining every power of my mind in investigating the Roman history from its beginning to the times of the tyranny, in all the remains of ancient authors that I could procure. This work gave me a deep and living insight into Roman antiquity, such as I never had before, and such as made me perceive, at the same time, clearly and vividly, that the representations of all the moderns, without exception, are but mistaken, imperfect glimpses of the truth. (p. 141)

He focused his study on 'the Roman laws of property, and the history of the Agrarian laws'. These early studies would form the basis of his lectures in Berlin. His *Römische Geschichte (Roman History)* was published in two volumes in 1811 and 1812, drawn from these lectures. In his book,

Niebuhr describes the history of Rome from its earliest times to the second century A.D., because, as he states, the Roman history by the English historian Edward Gibbon (1737–1794) commences from that point.

Niebuhr focuses on the expansion of Rome's empire, its wars within and outside Italy, the functioning of its administrative apparatus, and the legislation, customs, and the moral education (*Bildung*) of the Romans. He also applied the historicist principle, first formulated by Herder, that each epoch had to be understood in its own terms. Niebuhr emphasizes the need to look at the world of the Romans through their eyes. Clothing, the interior of houses, ships, food, trade, and agriculture were not what his listeners and readers might have expected: They would see the Romans filtered through ideas and practices familiar in their own time, rather than those that the Romans themselves had known. The same applies to the ideas that lay at the basis of Roman legislation, their institutions and their administrative apparatus, all of which were different from those in his time. Previous authors who had written about Rome – Niebuhr mentions Machiavelli (1469–1527) and Montesquieu (1689–1755) – had ignored the specificity of land ownership in ancient Rome, and understood its legislation from the perspective of the laws and institutions of their own time. He also accuses them of partiality in their admiration of Rome and its institutions. The academic historian had to be impartial. There is, Niebuhr admits, reason for deep admiration, especially for the republic and its laws, but there is also cause for abhorrence. Here Niebuhr is thinking of:

> the insatiable urge to rule, the unscrupulous contempt for the rights of strangers, the numb indifference to the suffering

of strangers, the greed, although looting was alien to them, and the separation of classes, from which not only towards slaves or strangers, but also towards fellow citizens often an inhuman heartlessness arose. (p. 13)

Niebuhr also criticizes the destruction of the Etruscan civilization by the Romans and draws a parallel between the Etruscans and the Aztecs, whose culture was destroyed by the Spaniards nearly two millennia later.

Philological and linguistic research methods allowed Niebuhr to discover the individuality of Roman society. Research into ancient languages, philology, had developed rapidly since the Renaissance. By the time Niebuhr began his studies, it formed the foundation of historical studies. But Niebuhr did something new when he asserted that philology had to strip the terms still used in his time from their current associations. In this way, he used philology to describe both the specificity of the past and what had changed over time.

With Niebuhr and Ranke, history became a critical academic discipline. Like Niebuhr, Ranke emphasized that the historian should be impartial, study sources critically, adhere strictly to the truth, and focus on what had been done: In short, the historian should focus on the facts (*Tatsachen*). For Ranke, historians should also direct their attention to finding *coherence* in the progression (*Fortgang*) of history – the form of the whole, as Niebuhr called it. The study of the sources alone presents the historian with mere fragments of that history. Finally, for Ranke, the practice of history is the study of the ethos of the nation as it is reflected in its customs, legislation, and institutions.

In his first book, *Geschichten der Romanischen und Germanischen Völker von 1494 bis 1514*, published in 1824, he wrote the following on the Latin and Germanic peoples:

> They are from the same or closely related tribes, similar in custom, having many institutions in common; their inner histories are closely interrelated, and they have several large undertakings in common. (pp. xv–xvi)

Typically historicist in this excerpt is the attention paid to customs and institutions, and the focus on the internal development of nations. The undertakings that Ranke refers to are the *Völkerwanderung*, the Crusades, and the colonization of foreign continents. Strikingly, in the description of these developments, Ranke does not, in contrast to Niebuhr, have an eye for the suffering and injustice these movements caused. Instead, he emphasizes how the Crusades, for instance, inspired the chivalric romance, 'the noble flower of chivalrous life'.

The events he mentions in this context are all part of one or other of these undertakings and thus are discussed in the light of them. Such is the typical historicist view of events. Events do not stand on their own: They occur in time and contribute to some undertaking or development. Historicists would say that events are an expression or manifestation of some underlying idea or historical *form*. This historicist 'theory of ideas' is best known from Humboldt's formulation of it. By carefully studying events, he wrote in his 1821 *Über die Aufgabe des Geschichtsschreibers* (*On the Task of the Historian*), the historian is able to extract the underlying ideas that necessitated those events and their outcomes. Such is the task of historians: They have to represent 'the struggle of an idea to realize itself in reality'. Think, for instance, of the ideas underlying the Crusades, of which the events that make up the Crusades are a realization. The effect of an event, the historicist says, only becomes evident afterwards. And that effect determines its historical meaning or significance. A truly *historical* moment has a decisive effect on later events. The individuals whose actions have such an effect are, according to Ranke, the most powerful minds on which the future rests.

To Ranke, history as an academic discipline was founded on the systematic research of primary sources. This still holds true for modern historians. They must compare multiple sources for the same event and determine which sources are reliable and why, what their function was, and how they can best be analysed. Historians must determine whether they are dealing with official documents or not, and whether those documents are genuine or counterfeit. They must determine who created the source so that it becomes clear how the views and intentions of its maker have coloured the information the source contains. They must also determine whether a source originated close to the events in time and place with which it is concerned, because the further away in time and place it is, the less reliable it is likely to be.

Ranke is also known for the introduction of the seminar: A class in which students – all male in Ranke's days – present their own work, after which the professor comments on it. Source criticism plays an important part in this. To this day, this method remains the ideal educational model for history students after they have successfully completed their introductory courses. Source criticism was not new in itself – think of philology. But the archives that Ranke managed to consult, and his use of them, made him the influential historian he came to be. The American historian Anthony Grafton (*b.* 1950) puts it thus:

> Earlier historians did not anticipate Ranke's ability to bring the flavor and texture of the documents into his own text. When Ranke used account books, ambassadorial dispatches and papal diaries to characterize the austere, wilful, and determined Franciscan who became Pope Sixtus V, and rebuilt the city of Rome into a magnificent stage for Catholic festivals and triumphal procession, he made his book into a sort of archive. He enabled the reader to share something of the impact of his own direct encounter with the sources. (p. 57)

This 'ability to bring the flavor and texture of the documents into his own text' also points to something else. The historian should aim to present the past *vividly*. Historians should use literary techniques for that purpose and to see coherence – an orderly whole – in the manifold of events, as long, of course, as those techniques are subordinated to his research. For Ranke and his fellow historicists at the start of the nineteenth century such as Niebuhr and Humboldt, history was both a science and an art.

Against Exemplary History

No two moments are ever the same, Herder wrote in his 1774 *Auch eine Philosophie der Geschichte* (*Also a Philosophy of History*). This is why there is nothing to be learned from past examples. This view would become a formative historicist principle. One by one, the historicists of the early nineteenth century would reject the exemplary theory of history. They particularly opposed eighteenth-century historiography and its view that one could draw general principles and lessons for the future from the past.

In his *Über die Aufgabe des Geschichtsschreibers*, Humboldt stated that the past examples which were supposed to serve as models to be followed were of no use whatsoever. They are often misleading and rarely illuminating, he writes. Ranke, too, distances himself from the view that there are lessons to be drawn from the past. In the preface to his *Geschichten der Romanischen und Germanischen Völker*, he put it thus:

> One has given history the task to judge the past, in order that lessons for the future can be drawn from it. Such an exalted task is not what this research is based on: it just wants to show how it really was like [*wie es eigentlich gewesen*]. (p. vii)

Hegel also rejected exemplary history in his 1820s lectures on the philosophy of history, published as *Vorlesungen über die Philosophie der Geschichte*. Examples of good behaviour may be instructive for children, so that they know what good and excellent behaviour is, but each time is characterized by its own specific (*eigentümliche*), individual circumstance. He adds:

> In the hustle and bustle of events on the world stage, a general ground rule is of no help, nor is the remembrance of what is similar; such a pale memory has no force whatsoever in comparison to the liveliness and freedom of the present. (p. 45)

Relying on historical examples, as for instance the French relied on Greek and Roman examples during the French Revolution, was therefore absurd. 'Nothing is more different than the nature of these peoples and the nature of our time.'

(p. 45) The only thing that history teaches us, he concludes, is that peoples and governments have never learned anything from it.

All this does not mean that knowledge of the past was an end in itself for the historicists. To Humboldt, the university had to be at the service of the nation. To that end, it should stimulate *geistigen und sittlichen Bildung*: Intellectual and moral education – a task which the university could only fulfil when the state guaranteed the academic freedom of research. The purpose of historical studies was to acquire a better grasp of reality, which was achieved through the knowledge of the 'forms' underlying past events. Ranke was more concrete. He argued that the purpose of historical knowledge was to support politics. This was the theme of his inaugural address when he advanced to a full professorship in Berlin in 1836. He writes:

> Therefore it is the task of history to discern the nature of the state from the sequence of earlier occurrences and bring to an understanding that which politics, after successive understanding and the gaining of insight, further develops and brings to fulfilment. (pp. 288–289)

This does not mean that history offers lessons for the future. Every circumstance is always different; the state is constantly evolving. But knowing how the present came to be and how it is part of some development, makes it clear where one stands and where one is headed, and allows the politician to decide what to do in relation to that development. The tasks of the historian and the usefulness of his work for the politician, as Ranke puts it here, are in line with the historicist view that the state, with its legislation, customs, and institutions, is the embodiment of the ethos of the nation. History in the nineteenth century is, for this reason, primarily political history.

Universal History

The 'historical school' to which Niebuhr, Savigny, Humboldt, and Ranke belonged, and the 'philosophical school' led by Hegel, disagreed about *how* the past should be studied. But there was much these historicists had in common.

They agreed that the study of the past should focus on the ethos of a nation, its moral life, as it is expressed in its habits, customs, and institutions. They also agreed that there is one history of humanity, that is, one universal history of the world, and that it occurs only once. This is how Ranke ends the preface of his first book:

> The main subject [of history-writing] is always [...] humanity as it is, explicable or inexplicable: the lives of individuals, the families [*Geschlechter*], the peoples, and at times the hand of God above them. (p. viii)

His book, however, as the title already indicates, was not concerned with universal history but with the history of the Latin and Germanic peoples. But these two forms of history are not incompatible. Specific to the historicist conception of universal history is that this history consists of nations, their internal development, and the influence they exerted upon each other. At some point, the history of humanity takes shape from within Europe, because the Europeans ensured the contact between nations, which is how individual histories of nations became connected and part of the history of mankind as a whole. In Ranke's view in his first book, this was done through the Crusades and then through the colonization of foreign continents. To Hegel, it was the European discovery of the idea that man as man is free which gave developments in Europe coherence and universal significance.

But what philosophy adds to the study of the past according to Hegel, and which historical studies lack, is the idea that the world-historical process is rational, that is, intelligible (*vernünftig*). The historians opposed this view and argued that the course of history – and its intelligibility – cannot be determined *a priori*: Only the close and critical investigations of documentary evidence, from which the historian infers what has been done, is able to show how nations developed internally over time and how they contributed to the history of mankind as whole.

To Hegel, history is the process in which *Geist* ('spirit') comes to understand itself. With spirit, he refers to self-aware man, who knows that he thinks and what he thinks. In becoming self-aware, man discovers that he is free, and such freedom, Hegel argues, can only be realized in a constitutional state, whose laws are acknowledged by its citizens as theirs. The history of the world, according to Hegel, is nothing but the spirit becoming aware of its freedom and trying to realize that freedom in the state, which, to Hegel, is a moral world. The course of history that thus emerges and which necessarily has a certain direction is, for Hegel, also a means to understand providence. For Hegel, as for his fellow historicists, providence coincides with the course of history.

History, in all parts of the world, starts with the emergence of states and their laws. But it was the Germanic peoples under the influence of Christianity who were the first to see that man as man is free, and that the state (with its laws), was a realization of man's desire for freedom. The Greeks and the Romans with their slave-based societies only knew that some were free. The states in the oriental world, Hegel contends, only admitted that their leaders were free; its subjects could not conceive of its laws as theirs, since laws existed only as a means of coercion.

Perhaps the most difficult aspect of Hegel's view of history is that the spirit of an individual and that of a people coincide.

> The spirit of a people [...] exists in its religion, in its cult, in its customs, its constitution and political laws, in the entirety of its rules, in its events and deeds. (p. 131)

Self-conscious individuals, Hegel says, appropriate these aspects of social and political life: It is their religion, their customs, their laws, and it is their people who have experienced this or that in the past. In this way, individuals are aware of themselves as members of a community, a people, and that is how the spirit of that people is present in individuals and thus coincides with them. If one then studies the work of a particular historical individual, such as a Roman historian, for instance, one will find the Roman spirit in that historian, inasmuch as that historian presents his views in terms of the spirit of his people. It follows that criticizing such a work and separating its facts from its fabrications, as Niebuhr did, means applying an understanding to the work alien to its spirit. This is why Hegel was critical of such reflective histories.

Difficult to understand, too, is the view that history is rational in the sense of being intelligible (*vernünftig*). Hegel does not deny that individuals are often guided by their passions, ambitions, and self-interests. But what is incomprehensible, irrational, or unreasonable at one moment, can still be in accordance with the spirit of its time, which makes it rational, that is, intelligible, at the level of the historical process. The individual is usually unaware of the development of the spirit. Reason may even be *cunning*, Hegel says, and trick the individual into doing its bidding, without him being aware of it. Only in the exceptional case of great men, of world-historical individuals, whose actions and thoughts are the best of their time, do the course of history and conscious action coincide, because those individuals know what their time is ripe for.

An Idiographic Science

History, according to late-nineteenth historicists, is an idiographic science. Such a science describes what is specific (*eigen*) to societies, their customs, habits, laws, and institutions, and their development in time. This is in contrast to the natural sciences, which are nomothetic sciences: Sciences that are based on laws, after the Greek word for law, *nomos*.

In the second half of the nineteenth century, positivists argued that history, too, should become a nomothetic science – which we mentioned in the first chapter of this book. Like the historicists and Nietzsche, the German philosopher Wilhelm Windelband (1848–1915) was of the opinion that a nomothetic historical science of societies would only produce trivial commonplaces about human behaviour. In addition, he opposed the positivists with the argument that they failed to recognize that everything of *value* is based on its uniqueness, and that it was precisely this uniqueness with which historical studies should be concerned. In his 1894 rectorial address, Windelband states:

Our very sense of value is rooted in the uniqueness [*Einmaligkeit*], the incomparability of all things.

When we think of our loved ones and our own lives, this view is immediately plausible:

Is it not an unbearable thought that a loved one, a venerated being, somewhere else also exists in the same way? Is it not frightening, unthinkable, that a second copy of ourselves with our individual individuality [*individuellen Eigenart*] would be present in this reality?

The idea of a *doppelgänger* is, in short, extremely unsettling, as Windelband observes:

How horrible is the thought that I as the same have already once lived and suffered, strived and fought, loved and hated, thought and wanted and that [...] I have to play this role again and again in the same theatre! And what applies to individual human life, that applies above all to the entire historical process: it only has value when it exists only once. (p. 36)

Just as the existence of individuals is unique and incomparable, so, too, is the entire historical process. It is precisely this uniqueness and incomparability of existence that makes life valuable, and makes it worthy of studying.

The emphasis on the temporal, singular existence in time of human beings as the foundation of historical studies is as old as history-writing itself, as we saw in the previous chapter. But to the historicists, nations and even the historical process itself also exist singularly in time. Windelband gives a specific twist to the debate about what kind of science history is by positing the uniqueness and incomparability of human existence as the condition for something being valuable. Therefore, history must be an idiographic science.

With the emphasis on what is specific and unique, Windelband does not deny that the idiographic sciences can rely on general knowledge and laws – quite the contrary. Historians always make use of that knowledge in their studies. This usually involves general knowledge of people's behaviour, which is indispensable in any historical research. But, Windelband emphasizes, historians must always bear in mind that their main concern is the representation of what singularly exists in time.

Windelband's rectorial address is widely known for its methodological distinction between idiographic and nomothetic sciences. The first focuses on specificity and individuality, on what is unique and singular, on forms (*Gestalten*) of life, while the second focuses on the general and what repeats itself, on what is abstract and general, on laws (*Gesetze*).

With the methodological distinction between idiographic and nomothetic sciences, he criticized the distinction between the sciences that was based on their subject matter 'nature' and 'mind' (*Geist*). That distinction cannot properly categorize psychology, which was a new, emerging discipline at the end of the nineteenth century. Psychologists examine the mind, but they do so in a nomothetic manner, says Windelband. The option of calling psychology a 'natural science of the mind' or a 'natural science of the inner sense' merely shows how unhelpful the distinction between nature and mind is, and how unfounded its associated distinction between the study of observable phenomena (*äussere Wahrnehmung*) and the study of the inner experience of perception (*innere Wahrnehmung*). All sciences, the natural sciences and the historical sciences, to use Windelband's preferred term for the humanities, are empirical sciences.

The principle of the individuality of individuals *and* of historical developments, and the opposition to the idea of modelling history in the image of the natural sciences, justify considering Windelband a historicist. But he didn't embrace the doctrine wholeheartedly. One consequence of historicism was the idea that values are historically conditioned. But if there are no universal, absolute, and always-valid values, how then do we know what is good and just?

The question of the relativism of values at the end of the nineteenth and the beginning of the 20th centuries led to the so-called 'crisis of historicism'. One solution was to posit the idea that the historical process itself showed which values are right and which are not. But this view could not be reconciled with the catastrophe that was the First World War. How could the state be the embodiment of the ethos of the nation when European states had sent a whole generation to die in a war for a cause which afterwards no one was able to recall? The organic unity which the moral life was believed to bring to the nation did not agree with nineteenth- and 20th-century parliamentary party democracy. This realization in Germany, where parliamentary democracy was established relatively late, in the aftermath of the war, further deepened the 'crisis of historicism'. It became obvious that the historicist conception of the nation was untenable.

In Chapter 5 we will return to the question of the relativism of values. But before we do so we need to delve deeper into the question of historical explanation.

4. Reasons and Causes

Historians not only describe past events but also seek to explain them. How historians do this is usually discussed in the context of the distinction between the sciences and the humanities. This is also the case with the philosopher of science Carl Hempel (1905–1997) in a much-discussed article from 1942 that deals with the function of laws in history-writing. He starts his article by remarking that it is often claimed that historians are concerned with describing particular events rather than with subsuming them under general laws. Therefore, so that argument goes, history is a different kind of discipline than the sciences. The distinction between describing particular events and subsuming them under general laws is, however, misleading, according to Hempel. Laws have a similar function in history as in the sciences. Events do not just happen; rather, there is a scientific explanation for them. His argument is rather straightforward. To *explain* is to reveal causes behind consequences; only a law can connect cause and consequence; therefore, when historians explain, they use laws. Laws are universal hypotheses that can be confirmed or disconfirmed by empirical evidence. They make evident why a certain cause leads to a certain consequence.

This argument is not easily refuted. Hempel knows that historians often explain concrete events that have occurred only once, at one particular moment in time. For this reason, they usually offer no more than an explanation sketch, he says. Historians, he continues, thus provide an indication of the type of circumstance that necessarily leads to the type of events for which they seek an explanation. Further empirical research should reveal whether a more detailed explanation can be given. This further elaboration is usually provided by one of the social sciences. Historians therefore should make use of social-scientific findings. These may be concerned with causal relations that are not *necessary* but *probable*: They are the kind of relations that are based on statistical research.

Hempel supports his argument with several examples, including the following one:

> Consider, for example, the statement that the Dust Bowl farmers migrate to California 'because' continual drought and sandstorms render their existence increasingly precarious, and because California seems to them to offer so much better living conditions. This explanation rests on some such universal hypothesis as that populations will tend to migrate to regions which offer better living conditions. But it would obviously be difficult accurately to state this hypothesis in the form of a general law which is reasonably well confirmed by all the relevant evidence available. (pp. 40–41)

This passage illustrates the primary concern of Hempel's article. The *event* in need of *explanation* is the behaviour of a group of people at a particular moment in time: that is, the migration of Dust Bowl farmers to California in the 1930s. The circumstance of constant drought and dust storms on the prairie plains is the cause of deteriorating living conditions, and as such is also the cause of the resulting emigration. The general disposition (or tendency) of people to migrate to regions with better living conditions explains the emigration and links the cause with its consequence.

Observations such as these are common in historical studies. The few examples that Hempel offers in his article all concern such dispositional explanations. He is constantly concerned with the regularity of behaviour in certain circumstances, and therefore with the social-psychological or economic explanation of such behaviour. People tend to migrate to places with better living conditions. They do not want to lose their job, their home, their social status, their personal relations, and relinquish the influence they might have, the power they exert, and so forth.

It is often difficult to formulate the universal hypothesis in such a way that it is confirmed by all the empirical evidence. Also, universal hypotheses are often so self-evident that no effort is made to investigate them further. That populations tend to migrate to areas that offer better living conditions is such a self-evident universal hypothesis. But that does not alter the fact that historians use such hypotheses to explain events, even when they mention concrete causes for concrete consequences or identify a certain difference or similarity as a causal factor, revealed through a comparison. After all, only a law or a statistical relation can connect cause and effect. Moreover, when historians explain a complex phenomenon such as the Dust Bowl, and cite several causes for it, they use universal hypotheses, for there may well be several laws or statistical relations at play which together constitute a sufficient explanation for this complex event. Although there is only one period in history known as the Dust Bowl, the events that we associate with it can only be explained with the help of universal hypotheses. To explain is to use a general hypothesis.

There is, however, a problem which Hempel ignores. If we were to ask an individual farmer why he migrates to California, he would probably point out the droughts

Figure 3. *Abandoned Dust Bowl Home*. Photographer: Dorothea Lange, between 1935 and 1940.

and dust storms, and his disposition to migrate to an area with better living conditions. But those circumstances and disposition would not be *causes* but *reasons* for him to emigrate. Individuals think about what it is that they do: They reason and give reasons. The explanation based on reasons is therefore called the rational or intentional explanation of action. Historians explain behaviour and actions on the basis of circumstances, dispositions *and* reasons.

This chapter is concerned with the distinction between causes and reasons in historical studies, with the distinction between the so-called dispositional and rational explanation of behaviour and actions, and why the one explanation cannot be reduced to the other. Attention is also given to the explanation of irrational behaviour.

History as a Science of the Mind

In his article, Hempel devotes only one passage to reasons. He discusses the idea that knowledge of reasons results from the empathic powers of the historian. And empathizing with others is not a scientific method. At best it gives an initial indication of what may have been the case. Empathy is nothing but a heuristic tool. Hempel also wonders whether we can truly empathize with everyone. Is it really possible to empathize with a farmer during one of the heavy dust storms, and feel his fear, doubt, and desperation? Hempel's criticism is sound. In most cases our own life experience is so remote from that of the people in the past whose behaviour we aim to understand that any empathic identification is simply impossible. But historians who explain behaviour by means of reasons do not do so on the basis of their empathic abilities. They are not concerned with what Herder once called *Einfühlen*, the feeling into another mind and period, as Hempel suggests. Historians analyse the perspective from which individuals came to their actions, given their situation, their beliefs, and their motives. That is how historians understand historical individuals' actions, and they support their analysis with evidence. They therefore use scientific methods: systematic steps to arrive at statements that are justified given the available evidence.

Since individuals deliberate – they reason – the explanation of behaviour does not exhibit the empirical regularity or universality Hempel wants it to, as will become clear. The argument with which Hempel advocates for the *unity of science* is therefore unwarranted. Laws have the same function in history as in the natural sciences: They connect causes with their consequences. But historians are also interested in reasons. And that makes them humanities scholars.

It is sometimes said that when historians focus on the reasons that individuals had, they do not *explain* the behaviour but *understand* it. *Erklären* ('explaining') in the natural sciences then is opposed to *verstehen* ('understanding') in the humanities. But philosophers just as often state that giving reasons is a form of explanation too. If we understand why an individual did what he or she did, we also have an explanation for it. The distinction between explaining and understanding is thus not that substantive in this respect. It is also true that historians are concerned not only with the reasons for individuals to act and their deliberations but also in circumstances and dispositions and how they influence behaviour. Circumstances, dispositions, *and* reasons may explain behaviour. Depending on the questions the historian asks, the emphasis is one explanation rather than the other.

Explanations of behaviour based on circumstances, dispositions, or reasons can coexist without excluding one another. In one description behaviour is causal and regular, while it is rational in another description. But the attention to reasons is what makes the historian a humanities scholar, a scientist of the mind (*Geisteswissenschaftler*).

Hempel only has an eye for the necessity or probability of behaviour. In a certain circumstance and given certain dispositions, it is necessary or probable that people will behave in a certain way. With that he ignores important advice from the philosopher Immanuel Kant (1724–1804):

> It is just as impossible for the subtlest philosophy as for the commonest human reason to ratiocinate freedom away. Thus the latter must presuppose that no true contradiction

is encountered between freedom and the natural necessity of precisely the same human actions, for it can give up the concept of nature just as little as it can that of freedom. (p. 72)

Kant's advice is still relevant today. It helps us understand what historians do when they explain past actions and behaviour. They pay attention to circumstances, dispositions, and the freedom of individuals to act. But what is freedom? This question deserves a book of its own. I will suffice with the following. Freedom is being with yourself, as Hegel once put it: 'Free am I, when I am with myself.' Being with yourself is being self-aware. Because you are with yourself, you can give *reasons* for what you do and say, commit yourself to an act, and bear responsibility for it.

In his article Hempel totally discards this idea of 'being with yourself'. He thereby overlooks that man is both a natural, *sentient* (sensory) being, and a moral, *sapient* (thinking) being. As a natural and sentient being, humans stand in a *causal* relationship to their environment. The environment is the cause of sensory, empirically experienced impressions – a human being smells, tastes, sees, hears, and feels – and a human being can causally affect that environment through his body: For example, by using agricultural methods he may deplete the earth's soil. As a thinking and moral being, human beings stand in a *rational* relationship to their environment: They think about the sensory impressions they experience, and those impressions play a role in their deliberations and the responsibility they bear for what they do. Such is what the (empirically) observed droughts and dust storms are for the individuals involved. To the extent that human beings think about what they perceive, in relation to themselves and their actions, they are with themselves and therefore free.

Historians explain actions and behaviour based on: (i) the circumstances in which people find themselves; (ii) the nature of human beings and their dispositions, innate and learned; and (iii) the deliberations that they make and the beliefs and attitudes underlying these deliberations. Each type of explanation allows for a sense of freedom as being with yourself.

Freedom and Necessity

Specific dispositions explain how the droughts and dust storms on the plains in the United States may have come about in the 1930s. In his celebrated 1979 book *Dust Bowl: The Southern Plains in the 1930s*, the historian Donald Worster (*b.* 1941) writes:

> There was nothing in the plains society to check the progress of commercial farming, nothing to prevent it from taking the risks it was willing to take for profit. That is how and why the Dust Bowl came about. (p. 7)

There may be other explanations why land is misused, but, he adds:

> The American Dust Bowl of the thirties suggests that a capitalist-based society has a greater resource hunger than others, greater eagerness to take risks, and less capacity for restraint. (p. 7)

The same dispositions explain, according to Worster, both the Wall Street Crash of 1929 and the subsequent Depression. The crash, too, was the result of the dispositions that characterize a capitalist-based society. Such is the main argument of Worster's book.

Here, on the one hand, given (learned) dispositions, the individual is not free to do as he pleases. The disposition explains why individuals behave the way they do. Taking risks in order to make as much profit as possible explains the unrestrained methods of agriculture that depleted the soil and caused the Dust Bowl. But, on the other hand, insofar as individuals think about the circumstances in which they find themselves, and are self-aware of their dispositions, they are free in relation to those circumstances and dispositions, in the sense that they are with themselves. The explanation of behaviour based on dispositions therefore does not preclude the conception of freedom as being with yourself.

That a particular person decides to migrate at a certain moment in time can be explained by pointing to the disposition to realize better living conditions for his or her family. According to Hempel, such an explanation is based on the universal hypothesis that people migrate to areas offering better living conditions. The emigration can also be explained by pointing to the circumstances of droughts and dust storms, which made life more difficult or even impossible, forcing farmers to migrate. These individuals were also not free to do what they wanted, according to this explanation. In that circumstance, as thinking, autonomous beings, they are also able not only to observe the droughts and dust storms, but also to accept that they must either migrate or not. They conceive of what they have perceived in a certain way and let it play a role in the deliberations they make. In this ability to reason about the situation they are in, they find their freedom.

For some scholars, the individual who is self-aware is central to history-writing and historical thinking. One such

Figure 4. *Dust Bowl Refugees Reach a 'Promised Land' – California /'A Family Unit in the Flight From Drought'.* Photographer: Dorothea Lange, 1936.

scholar is the archaeologist and philosopher Robin Collingwood (1889–1943). He puts it this way in his posthumously published *The Idea of History*:

> All history is the history of thought; and when an historian says that a man is in a certain situation this is the same as saying that he thinks he is in this situation. The hard facts of the situation, which it is so important for him to face, are the hard facts of the way in which he conceives the situation. (p. 317)

Collingwood would emphasize that there is history only insofar as emigration is explained with reference to the thoughts of the individuals involved, and the intentions and beliefs they had at that moment. Here, individuals are with themselves – they are self-aware – because they are able to make evident to themselves and to others why they act as they do. The droughts and dust storms that caused the deteriorated living conditions then are reasons for a person to behave in a certain way.

Collingwood seems to have little regard for dispositions and their role in the explanation of behaviour. And circumstances are only relevant to the historian when there is a person involved who can conceive of the situation in a certain way. It thus appears that the historian, in Collingwood's view, is only concerned with individuals, since only individuals have thoughts and think about the situation they are in. Clearly, this is not the only thing that interests the historian. The protagonists in history are often social groups, cities, nations, states, or regions of the world. The attention to individuals in history-writing is always connected to the society in which those individuals lived, and the social, economic, and political circumstances in which they found themselves. Such circumstances are not ignored by Collingwood. Nor does Collingwood simply ignore dispositions outright. But there is only history when dispositions can be related to thoughts, when these thoughts denaturalize dispositions and turn them into rational decisions, and when the thought processes of individuals are related to society and its existing social habits. Collingwood says:

> The historian is not interested in the fact that men eat and sleep and make love and thus satisfy their natural appetites: but he is interested in the social customs which they create by their thought as a framework within which these appetites find satisfaction in ways sanctioned by convention and morality. (p. 216)

The dispositions with which Worster explains the Dust Bowl would, according to Collingwood, point to capitalism as an idea – as the spirit of a society, as Hegel would have it. As an idea, capitalism is the framework from which dispositions and the behaviour resulting from them such as making profit, taking risks, and having a hunger for resources, become intelligible.

We often explain and predict behaviour on the basis of the circumstances causing that behaviour and our knowledge of dispositions and the behaviour that results from them. Explanations of this kind are common to both historical studies and the social sciences. One could argue that history *is* a social science inasmuch as it explains behaviour with reference to circumstances and dispositions. That's the argument of 20th-century positivists such as Hempel, who claim that universal hypotheses in historical studies have a similar function to universal hypotheses in the sciences. This view is opposed by the argument that what individuals think about what they do, their considerations, beliefs, intentions, and the reasons they have and are able to give, are part of the *portrait* of those individuals created by the historian. And that has nothing to do with the type of explanation privileged by the positivists. We may add that the rational explanation explains behaviour in a way in which the individuals under discussion would have understood their own behaviour.

Considerations such as these are typical of hermeneutically minded scholars. Their approach focuses on the meaning that individuals themselves attach to what they do and what they experience. In doing so, hermeneutists acknowledge the freedom of the individual, who is aware of the situation he or she is in, is 'with him- or herself', and can make decisions based on this. Despite this opposition between positivism and hermeneutics, we should realize that the types of explanation do not exclude each other and can coexist. Historians explain behaviour on the basis of circumstances, dispositions, and reasons.

This raises at least two questions. How exactly do we distinguish between the dispositional and rational explanation of behaviour? And is the rational explanation of behaviour able to account for *irrational* behaviour?

Dispositions and Reasons

Worster does pay some, albeit limited, attention to the deliberations of individuals. Of the farmers for instance he writes:

> Some remained out of sheer inertia or bewilderment over what else to do, or because they had the economic means to stay where others did not. Whatever the reason people had for not moving away, hope was commonly a part of them. The people were optimists, unwilling to believe that the dust storms would last or that their damage would be very severe. (p. 26)

Here, Worster speaks of reasons, thereby pointing to the rational explanation. Yet the difference between the dispositional and rational explanation is not immediately clear. If optimism offers an explanation for the behaviour, without the individual playing a role as a rational being in that explanation, then the explanation is a dispositional explanation. If the behaviour is explained on the basis of deliberations – the dust storms will cease and the damage will be small – then the explanation is a rational explanation, despite the fact that these deliberations can be characterized as forms of optimism. In the quoted passage, the two explanations are interwoven. This is very common in historical studies.

The passage also makes it clear that what may be rational for individuals themselves (the hope that everything will be all right) can be perceived as *irrational* by someone else (it would have been rational to migrate). The term 'rational explanation' is in this respect not very fortunate. This also becomes clear in another example offered by Worster:

> They [the plainsmen] are prouder of their ability to tough it out than to analyze their situation rationally, because they expect nature to be good to them and make them prosper. (p. 27)

Here, the explanations themselves are intertwined: Pride is a disposition, while expecting something points to a deliberation. The rational explanation does not state that people reason optimally, as if they are following an algorithm or are expert logicians. People often make assessments based on (unrealistic) expectations of what will happen in the future. That something is rational to do in a given circumstance does not explain why individuals in fact did what they did. Migrating may be the most rational thing to do in a certain situation, but individuals may still decide not to do so.

To explain why individuals behave the way they behave, we need to know what their deliberations and motives were (if our aim is to give a rational explanation for their behaviour, of course). These we find out by asking questions. This is the first rule of hermeneutics: What you aim to understand should be taken to be an answer to a question or a solution to a problem. How is it possible that some people stayed? Because they expected the tide to turn and nature to offer them riches again. With the answers we give to the questions we ask, we re-enact a person's thought process. This brings to the fore the inner connections between beliefs, motifs, and reasons. Collingwood calls it the *re-enactment of past thought*. What people do and bring forth not only has an *outside* that can be observed but also an *inside* that we can think again. This is not some miraculous placing of oneself literally in the mind of people in the past. It is the placing of oneself into the perspective under which people have come to their beliefs and reasons.

The rational explanation places the action to be explained in a context of beliefs, reasons, thoughts, judgements, intentions, and motives. In this case, the expectation was that the dust storms would pass, that the damage would not be severe, and that nature would be good and offer prosperity again. Being a rational person also includes being responsible and being able to bear responsibility and give justifications for one's actions. A rational being is, in other words, a moral being. She can justify, for herself and for others, by giving reasons, why she migrates or not, and thus can be held accountable for her actions.

The tragedy of human existence is not that actions often have unintended consequences. The tragedy is that such unintended consequences oppose the way of life that inspired the action in the first place. The Dust Bowl is a good example of this. The farmers were inclined to maximize profits, which was their motive for what they did. They did not *intend* to deplete the soil and thereby create dust storms. The Dust Bowl was an unintended consequence of a series of actions, which made their way of living impossible. Attending to both what is intended *and* unintended is an important aspect of historical research.

In explaining the Dust Bowl and its consequences, Worster is mainly interested in dispositions. This follows from the kind of history he writes. His work is a social history, in this case, the history of an ecological disaster. One of the dispositions that Worster is interested in is optimism, as we just saw. As a disposition, optimism is part of capitalist society: It is the ethos of a society that makes social elevation and improvement possible. But it can also be a strategy of survival or even a form of madness, and it can prevent people from self-reflection, thereby blocking substantial reforms. That was what happened on the plains, according to Worster. Optimism was an obstacle to making the right decisions.

The dispositional explanation tells us what certain dispositions are. It provides general knowledge of human beings and their behaviour. Such knowledge is indispensable in any historical study. The rational explanation, by contrast, makes it clear how individuals feel about what they do and the reasons they can give for doing so. It thereby provides knowledge of individuals and who they are. I argue that the rational explanation cannot be reduced to the dispositional explanation. This is in opposition to what the so-called behaviourists believe, who think that talking about the inner life of people is misleading. In addition, I assert that the two types of explanation, rational and dispositional, do not contradict one another but may coexist.

Subjects

One critical comment has to be added to our discussion of the explanation of behaviour. In her 1991 article 'The Evidence of Experience', the American historian Joan Scott (*b.* 1941) argues that historians cannot appeal to the experiences of individuals as the ultimate grounds of the claims they make, for:

> It is not individuals who have experience, but subjects who are constituted through experience. (p. 779)

A person does not have experiences as an individual, but as a subject, as a black man, a white woman, a farmer, a migrant, or an ecologist, for instance. Scott underlines that subjects are constructed by society and that they change over time. Therefore, we should historicize the experience of being a subject by studying how subjects and subjectivities are made.

Each category of subjects includes behaviour that is characteristic and perceived as socially accepted and appropriate or not. Individuals tend to behave according to the category under which they fall, as defined by themselves and society. Thus, a plainsman behaves as a plainsman should behave. Categories of subjects allow for self-understanding, and hence for subjectivity, which is not to say that one cannot resist the assumptions of the category under which one falls, struggle for the acceptance of (certain of) its characteristics, or fight for rights withheld from one's category. Given what we have said about explanation, it follows that, when an explanation is offered of some action or behaviour, such categories of subjects and the processes by which they are created are to be taken into account, since each subject is associated with particular dispositions and reasons offered by individuals.

Worster does historicize experience, but he does not self-consciously analyse how subjects and subjectivities are constructed in ways that allow for individual experiences. He discusses changes in subjects and subjectivities in relation to the Dust Bowl which, for example, helped to bring about the ecologist, ecological science, and popular ecological works, and in its wake, encouraged institutions to represent the public's interest and stimulated planning of such things as land use. As such, one might say, the ecologist was 'discursively created' and became a subject acting upon other subjects, thereby establishing a new power relation. Worster writes:

> For all of these champions the emerging science was to be, first, an instructor in the laws of nature and, second, a servant of man, showing him how to exploit the land without destroying it, how to create, where necessary, a new system of checks and balances. (p. 201)

The analysis advocated by scholars such as Scott is known as post-structuralism. Behaviour and actions are not so much the results of societal structures, but are to be analysed as part of the discursive processes in which subjects and subjectivities are made.

Points of View

The farmers could not, of course, foresee the Dust Bowl, much less the significance it would acquire in Worster's work. Worster makes the droughts and dust storms on the plains in the 1930s a part of the history of the United States, as well as of Western capitalism and ecological awareness. He thereby assigns a certain historical significance to that episode, which only becomes clear in the story he tells after-wards. Such a perspective on the part of the historian cannot be inferred from the perspective of past individuals. In the past, people could not know what future historians would know. Their future was still open, while, to the historian, it is now foreclosed.

Worster states in his work that an ecological balance can only exist on the plains if something is done about the economic culture. This was a relatively new perspective at the time (the late 1970s) at which he wrote his book. Even though the Dust Bowl brought ecology to the attention of policymakers, the economic reforms needed to establish an ecological equilibrium had, up to this point, been ignored. In the afterword to the reprint of the book on the 25th anniversary of its publication, Worster writes:

> It [the book] did raise relatively new questions about how the modern market economy brought unprecedented environmental transformation, taught a new set of values toward the natural world, and not only deliberately risked capital for gain but also risked an already shaky ecological stability for short-term private advantage. (p. 246)

This summarizes the point of view from which he wrote his book. It is the thesis or conclusion he reached in it. This is how, the book tells us, one must look at that particular episode, the Dust Bowl, in American history. This is precisely what historians do. They propose interpretations of the past from a certain point of view, which allow for the coherence of the narratives they write. It should by now be clear that the historian is not just a chronicler collecting facts and putting them in chronological order.

The term 'Dust Bowl' has acquired a specific meaning through the work of Worster. It is no longer a term that stands for droughts and dust storms in the 1930s, but rather denotes everything that Worster has to say about it in his book. This gives the term a certain autonomy with regard to the past which it did not have before. To put it another way: It makes a difference whether we talk about droughts and dust storms or about droughts and dust storms *from the point of view of Worster's book*. In his 1981 dissertation *Narrative Logic*, of which a revised edition was published in 1983, the Dutch historian and philosopher of history Frank Ankersmit (*b*. 1945) proposed speaking of 'narrative substances' in the case of the latter. The narrative substance in the work of the historian ensures that everything that is said about the past in that work is understood from the point of view proposed in that work.

Such proposals to view the past in a certain way are, among other things, characterized by the political and moral standards of the author. Worster's analysis of the functioning of capital is Marxist. But Karl Marx himself (1818–1883) did not pay attention to ecology. Worster's aim was therefore to integrate the Marxist economic analysis with an ecological analysis. This combination made his specific point of view possible, which is itself historically conditioned and first emerged at that time. With his analysis, Worster offered a perspective on contemporary problems in his own day. Here, it is important to note that the political and moral standards of the historian enable a certain kind of history-writing (we made that observation earlier, in Chapter 2). This can also make it clear what history's relevance is, as we will find out in the next chapter.

5.   Historical Insight

According to Ankersmit, political and moral views play a positive role in the discipline of history. He offers two reasons for this. First, the political and moral standards of the historian provide the kind of historical writing with which we can orient ourselves to both the present and future. Second, such history-writing allows us to determine what the right and wrong political and moral standards are. With these two reasons, Ankersmit points to two important functions of history-writing. A historical study is not an end in itself. But how are we to conceive of this idea concretely?

Remember Worster's Marxist-ecological analysis, which we discussed in the previous chapter. His analysis allows us to conceive of economic behaviour in a capitalist society and the motives behind it in a certain way, in relation to natural resources and their exploitation. With his work we can orient ourselves to the present and let ecological considerations play a role in the opinions we have about the exploitation of agricultural land. We can also decide that certain ecological standards – a balance between nature and exploitation for instance – are the right standards. Another example is found in the work of Scott, who calls her work avowedly political: With her gender analysis, she examines the inequality between men and women in the past with the aim of changing that inequality in the present. Here, too, the political and moral views of the historian provide the kind of history-writing that offers a perspective on the present. The fact that Scott wants to combat inequalities in the present makes it clear that her work enables us to determine which political and moral standards are the right ones.

Ankersmit emphasizes that we, ideally, should possess several studies of the same historical phenomenon, written on the basis of different political and moral standards, in order to determine the merits and shortcomings of those standards in relation to one another. He thereby gives a specific explanation for the debates between historians and underlines their importance. Such debates are usually not about the past itself – the actual course of events and the evidence for it – but about the point of view from which the past is best understood. And it is not so much the end of the debate that is a mark of the discipline's vitality, but the continuation of the debate itself. For historians not only study the past but also study the history of history-writing. And they have to position themselves in relation to that history in their own work.

It is clear that history-writing has an obvious purpose for Ankersmit: It enables us to reflect on the society in which we live by providing perspectives on the present. This use also presupposes a specific conception of the nature of history as a discipline: It provides insight into the past. As I have suggested once or twice already, the answers to the questions of what history is and what its use is, are mutually dependent. This chapter focuses on the answers given by Ankersmit, arguably the most influential Dutch philosopher of history past or present, both in the Netherlands and abroad.

Subjectivity and Objectivity

Many will endorse the view that history is useful because it enables us to reflect on the society in which we live. But few would admit that the political and moral views of the historian have a positive role to play in this. After all, shouldn't the historian be objective? Should they not be impartial, erase themselves from their work, let the facts speak for themselves, and refrain from judging the past, as Ranke had demanded? Is that not what makes the work of the historian academic, accurate, and trustworthy? How are we to reconcile these demands on history as an academic discipline with the plea to make use of subjective political and moral standards in that discipline?

Ankersmit distinguishes, in this context, between the *cognitive* and *normative* functions of political and moral standards in history-writing. To the extent that these standards make a certain type of history-writing possible, they have a cognitive function: They highlight certain aspects of the past as they enable the historian to interpret that past from a certain point of view. Only that cognitive function has a positive role in historical studies. The Rankeans rightly fear and reject the normative function of political and moral standards, because that would make the work of the historian biased and partial, and thus susceptible to a distortion and ignorance of facts. Obviously, this is not what Ankersmit argues for. Historians are not to prescribe what the past should have been, given their political and moral views. They also are not to select only those facts that support their political and moral standards in order to serve certain interests in the present. The practice of history as a discipline is not, and should not be, normative and political in that sense. Worster's analysis may be Marxist, but his book is not a plea for a socialist state. Scott does combat inequalities between men and women in the present, but, to her, gender is a way of analysing the past, not the object of analysis. This is how gender and the political and moral standards related to it have a cognitive function: They enable her to write her histories. With the distinction provided by

Ankersmit, we can reconcile the *subjectivity* of the historian (the cognitive function of political and moral standards, which is to be praised) with the disciplinary requirement of *objectivity* (the normative function of those standards, which are to be rejected). Another example may further clarify the distinction between the cognitive and normative functions of political and moral standards in history-writing.

Ranke, too, understood the past from a certain standpoint. His perspective was shaped by his conservative views and basically boils down to the following. The idea of the nation, of national awareness, was, according to Ranke, the product of the Reformation and the wars of religion in the sixteenth and seventeenth centuries. The French Revolution was a final test to the European order. After that, the European powers had the common goal of maintaining the balance of power, allowing nations to continue to develop internally without being threatened by wars from the outside. Such was the natural outcome of history, in which the Europeans had managed to realize themselves in church and state. The European order in his own nineteenth century was thus the result of developments that had been initiated centuries earlier. These views betray Ranke's conservative point of view through which, in his work, events acquired coherence and meaning. This viewpoint has a *cognitive* function because it highlights certain aspects of the past, such as the rejection of everything that threatens the authority of church and state and their possible alternatives, and because it emphasizes the existing order as the natural outcome of history as it gradually unfolded. Ranke's conservatism has no normative function in his work because he is impartial, because he does not say what the past should have been like, and because he does not search for evidence to justify his conservative views, but he does interpret the past from a conservative point of view.

The Historicity of Moral Values

Ankersmit also notes that our political and moral values are historically conditioned. This is a much-repeated historicist proposition that we can accept. One of the things that history teaches us is that our moral values change over time and thus have a history. Think, for example, of universal suffrage. In the Netherlands, the right to vote was extended in 1917 to allow all men to vote. In 1919, women, too, were given that right. The right to vote without restriction of gender, wealth, and education is a democratic norm and value that is historically conditioned. The norm – everyone being allowed to vote – and value – that it is right that everyone is allowed to vote – came about *in* time, and did not happen without a struggle. Think also for example of patronage and clientage, a common practice in the early modern period, although it was rejected in modern times because it was believed not to be in agreement with the modern state. The political and moral values associated with patronage and clientage had changed. It is up to historians to make it clear how political and moral values function and change over time. I want to make two comments on the historicist view of norms and values.

First, there is a risk that we will not question the norms and values that we possess precisely because they *are* historically conditioned. At such moments we believe that we are such-and-such because we have become that way, and that this is also the way things were meant to be. But sometimes we have to be willing to shake off the past, to bring it to justice and condemn it, as Nietzsche argued (see Chapter 1). The fact that norms and values are historically conditioned does not mean that they are right.

Secondly, we must realize that although norms and values are historically conditioned, as the historicists rightly proclaim, we cannot help but hold the norms and values that we currently have to be universally valid. If we now reject patronage and clientage in our political system, we also reject the political and moral standards associated with it for other times, even though we know that it was thought about differently in other times. We do not say: It is right that in the early modern period patronage and clientage was the norm or that no one was allowed to vote. Nor do we say that tomorrow we will no longer reject patronage and clientage or embrace democracy – as long as we are convinced of course that patronage and clientage in our political system must be rejected and democracy should be embraced. *Having* certain norms and values is a different thing from *knowing* what certain norms and values are. We do not know which norms and values we will have in the future, and if we are convinced that a certain norm or value will be ours in the future, then that future has already presented itself and become present. Holding the norms and values that we currently have to be universally valid ensures our ability to judge both the present and the past, without implying that we ignore what is specific to that past.

Another point needs to be made. From the concrete facts of the past, we may infer what the right norms and values for our own time may be.

Facts and Values

The distinction between facts on the one hand and norms and values on the other is a distinction between what is and what should be, between the *is* and *ought*, or, as the

Germans have it, between *sein* and *sollen*. In theory, we distinguish facts from norms and values, but they often overlap in practice. When we hear that the earth is warming up, the suggestion is that this should not be the case. When we hear that the number of murders committed is decreasing, the suggestion is that this should be the case. What is (a fact) thus leads rather naturally to what should be (a norm to which a value is connected). The question is: Does this also hold true for the relationship between the past and the present? If knowledge of the past is useful in the present, then we can infer from what happened in the past how things ought to be in the present and the future. And, in practice, it often seems to work that way. When we read about war, slavery, and tyranny, most of us will think that these should not have happened, and that they should not happen again. We hear about altruism, self-sacrifice, and the struggle for justice, and we realize: This is how it should be in the present and the future. Almost naturally there is a continuity between facts and norms and values.

Ankersmit puts it thus in his 2001 essay 'In Praise of Subjectivity':

> As soon as we have to do with the unicity and the concreteness of individual historical contexts, this continuity between fact and norm immediately takes over, and the distinction between the 'is' and the 'ought' then is an artificial and unrealistic a priori construction. (p. 94)

Here, it is important to note that this continuity between fact and norm offers us a way to reflect on the usefulness of historical knowledge. Is it not the task of history to hold up a mirror to us, so that it becomes clear to us what should be avoided and done differently in our present? The historian offers us the facts of the past, and as readers and hearers we realize what ought to be the case – what norms and values are the right ones and should be pursued.

This way of putting things is, however, misleading because it suggests that the historian only has to represent the facts of the past as they have been: as if his or her primary task is simply to list the facts in their right chronological order. Ankersmit, by contrast, emphasizes that historians must come up with a *proposal* to view the past from a certain vantage point. The historian establishes facts and selects them based on the questions she asks and the methods available to her to infer those facts from the sources. Those facts first acquire meaning from the point of view proposed by the historian. And with that point of view, we can orient ourselves to the present and the future.

The Use of History

When we think of concrete historical situations, the continuity between fact and norm immediately takes over. But the historian does more than establish and select facts. One historian looks at the past from his or her point of view, a second from another. This is, according to Ankersmit, the ideal scenario. By comparing points of view, a historical debate is opened about the merits and shortcomings of those points of view and what they bring to light, and the political and moral standards on which they are based. The viewpoint that provides the most insight into the past will get the most supporters, and will therefore be the most successful. But how do we determine which viewpoint offers the most insight and is therefore the best? Ankersmit argues that the best viewpoint is the most fruitful, has the largest scope, provides the most consistent image, and is the most original. Based on those criteria, we can rationally discuss the merits and shortcomings of points of view in relation to each other. Therefore, history-writing, according to Ankersmit, is:

> The experimental garden where we may try out different political and moral values and where the overarching aesthetic criteria of representational success [such as scope, consistency, fruitfulness, and originality] will allow us to assess their respective merits and shortcomings. (p. 99)

Here, Ankersmit locates the usefulness of history-writing. The historian's point of view and this perspective's underlying political and moral values enable us to decide which political and moral values to prefer. We do not learn from the past nor from analogies between the present and the past. We learn from the insight that historical writing offers into the past: Such insight also helps us to orient ourselves to the present and the future. This is why history is useful. The *past* is not to be used to argue for or against a certain perspective on the present. But the *work of history* is. This also underlines the point that historical studies should be concerned with the society in which they are written.

This use of history does not depend on a specific part of the past being studied since what matters is the insight it offers. Nor is it dependent on the type of history being written. Points of view make certain aspects of political reality visible in the past. The term 'political reality' must be understood in a broad sense: It stands for the way in which society is organized and the struggle for influence on that organization. It consists not only of political elements, but also of cultural and socio-economic elements.

That we cannot learn anything from the past is a historicist claim, as we saw in Chapter 3. No two moments in the world are ever the same. Every circumstance is different. The nineteenth-century historicists, however, had less regard for the cognitive function of political norms and values, and how they enable a certain type of history that allows us to orient ourselves to the present and the future. These historians saw the usefulness of history principally in its revelation of the nature of the state and how that nature should be further developed through politics.

The emphasis on the continuity between facts and norms is not in conflict with historicism. When historicists claim that every circumstance is always different and that we therefore cannot learn anything from past events nor from the principles deduced from them, they have something else in mind. Nothing can be learned from the French Revolution in the sense that, given an (impending) revolution now, examples or principles from that time would be of no help to us. But in practice we automatically link the facts we know about the French Revolution to the values and norms that we now have.

With an emphasis on the cognitive function of the political and moral values with which history is written, and the political and moral values that we can in turn infer from reading such a history, Ankersmit not only makes it clear why history is useful, but also pleads for the historian to be *involved* in his subject matter. A historian's social and political interests determine the perspective from which the past is interpreted.

The Interpretation of the French Revolution

I will further clarify Ankersmit's argument with the help of the introduction of Lynn Hunt's (*b.* 1945) well-known 1984 book *Politics, Culture, and Class in the French Revolution.* Hunt first distinguishes between three different interpretations of the French Revolution: the Marxist, the revisionist, and the interpretation of Alexis de Tocqueville (1805–1859). Then she adds her own interpretation. I will give a somewhat simplified account of each of these interpretations.

In the Marxist interpretation, things such as the liberal constitution, terror, democracy, and authoritarian power are nothing but the means of the bourgeoisie to bring themselves into and then to retain power, and with it, capitalism. For the liberal Tocqueville, these matters are part of the modernization of the state which is characterized by the expansion, centralization, and rationalization of state power. The revisionists turned against the Marxist interpretation: The Revolution was not caused by the class struggle between bourgeoisie and aristocracy. Some revisionists see the Revolution as an unnecessary and regrettable interruption of an otherwise gradual restructuring of the social and political order. In this we can recognize the conservative interpretation of the Revolution, whereby the Revolution plunged the institutions of church and state into a crisis that they barely survived. Other revisionists argued that the Revolution did not serve the interests of the bourgeoisie and capitalism at all, and that the Revolution was essentially reactionary.

Hunt emphasizes that all three interpretations focus on the origin and outcome of the Revolution. She no longer finds such a focus adequate because with it, the politics of the revolution itself falls out of view. It cannot provide insight into the revolutionary experience, and that is what Hunt's book is all about. She wants to restore the politics of the revolution to the foreground. Her own interpretation is strongly individualistic and liberal-democratic in the sense that she focuses on the diversity of revolutionary experiences among broad sections of the population and the way in which revolutionary awareness was expressed in the practices of everyday life. The thesis of her book is that the French Revolution was the beginning of a new political culture: The emergence of ideology, and that political culture was reflected in all of cultural life. Her perspective ensures a consistent view of the French Revolution and the political culture that first took shape during the Revolution. As such, it thereby has a cognitive function.

Here, it is important to note that Hunt discusses different interpretations in relation to one another and that those interpretations are points of view that are themselves based on political and moral values. These political and moral values make a certain interpretation possible and therefore have a cognitive function. The adequacy of those interpretations is discussed at the level of those points of view and not at the level of the facts or sources. In this way, Hunt positions her work within the history of history-writing.

Her book is typical of the 1980s. On the one hand, this is because at that time, within the discipline of history, a more anthropological approach to the past was in vogue – an approach that Hunt follows when she investigates cultural practices of daily life and the symbolism used therein. On the other hand, her book reflects the fact that in Western societies at the time, technology and prosperity had created an individualistic and liberal-democratic climate on which there was a broad political and social consensus. Hunt's interpretation of the Revolution is in the spirit of her time, as Hegel would have it.

The work of the historian thus originates in a certain time and itself becomes a part of history. This also means that Hunt and her readers, through her studies, become aware of their own day and age.

Historical Insight

The vantage point from which the historian looks at the past provides *insight* into that past. Insight is not the same as having knowledge of something. We need to develop insight, and then we can transmit that to others, learning how to view reality in a new way. Hunt's interpretation teaches us to view the Revolution in a different way. The questions that the historian asks lead to a certain selection of facts that may in part be new – Hunt, for example, discusses the fact that certain political preferences were visible in card games: This detail will not have been mentioned in other historical works. But the core of her book does not consist of the facts it mentions. The core is the insight that Hunt offers as to the implications of the Revolution. All the facts she mentions, the new and the old, are related to that insight: They become visible through it and they exemplify her thesis that the Revolution brought about a new political culture.

With the help of her insight, we can orient ourselves to the present and the future. We could, for example, focus our attention on the politics of cultural life in the present, and the diversity of today's political experiences. Insights such as these make history relevant, because such an insight enables us to think in a new way about our own political reality and about how we justify our political and moral actions. We can

Figure 5. Playing cards. Freedom of Religion and Equality Before the Law. Fabricated in 1793.

also conclude that individual liberal-democratic standards are preferable to other political and moral standards, or contemplate what its shortcomings are. The political and moral values of the historian thus have a positive function in history-writing because they offer us new perspectives. As such, the subjectivity of the historian, as Ankersmit argues, is something that we should praise.

Insight involves a different way of viewing that with which we are already familiar. In other words, at a certain moment the historian sees something *in* the past that was not visible previously. A good work increases our insight into the past, and its ability to do so constitutes the distinguishing merit of the individual historian whose task is in other words to tell us what he or she has learned rather than what has been proven. Every good historical work does that in its own particular way. This once again underlines the subjectivity of the historian. According to Ankersmit in his *Aesthetic Politics* from 1996, it requires talent or *virtù* to find the perspective that makes past political reality most visible. Here, Ankersmit reminds us of Nietzsche, who wrote in his *Vom Nutzen und Nachteil der Historie für das Leben*:

> Do not believe any historical writing if it does not issue from the head of the rarest minds [...]: the genuine historian must have the strength to recast the well known into something never heard before and to proclaim the general so simply and profoundly that one overlooks its simplicity because of its profundity and its profundity because of its simplicity. (p. 37)

One has to arrive at insight. And there is no specific procedure for that. As Nietzsche emphasizes, it appeals to the artistic capacities of the historian, to his or her creativity and intuition.

Ankersmit, too, arrives at this conclusion. There are, he argues, no rules through which the past can be translated into (or projected onto the level of) the historical work itself. To be sure, there are rules for the analysis and use of evidence. For example, the historian must compare sources with each other and determine whether a source is authentic or a forgery. There are also rules for writing a historical work. For example, the work must have a certain structure and be followable and consistent. But how historians arrive at the point of view through which they select and give coherence and meaning to the facts that they derived from their sources is something that cannot be captured in a procedure or 'method'. Every good historical work does so in its own unique way. And that points to the artistic, creative abilities of the historian. In other words, the historian designs his or her own unique rules to represent the past. We can call that individual way of representation the personal *style* of the historian. Finally, it is important that we realize that the historian's insight does not follow from the events in the past themselves and cannot be inferred from them. Historical studies do not mirror the past. They are proposals for understanding the past from a certain point of view.

The artistic ability or talent to arrive at a certain insight points to the role of aesthetics in historical practice. An important question here is how historians give shape to the past in their work. For Ankersmit, this means that we think about the *aesthetic* question of what an insight is, and with it what the scope, consistency, fruitfulness, and originality are as criteria to determine the merits and shortcomings of one insight compared with another. A completely different question is how the historical work relates to the past and the available evidence. That is an *epistemological* question which has to do with the way in which the historian acquires knowledge. These two different questions should not be confused with one another.

In terms of aesthetics, we wonder how Hunt has succeeded in representing the diverse revolutionary experiences and social circumstances in a coherent manner, and what the scope, consistency, fruitfulness, and originality of her representation is. Our epistemological interest is evident in our concern with how she represents cultural expressions, beliefs, political struggle, motives, and so forth, given the evidence that is available, the methods with which that evidence has been studied, the concepts she uses for that purpose, and the explanations she provides.

Ankersmit wants to defend a fundamental position with his views on history-writing. Since the insight of the historian requires artistic talent, after which her work enables us to orient ourselves to the present and the future and allows us to decide what the right and wrong political standards are, aesthetics precedes ethics.

Metahistory

In his 1973 book *Metahistory*, the American historiographer and philosopher of history Hayden White (1928–2018) arrives at similar conclusions to those of Ankersmit. Nineteenth-century historians and philosophers had conceptions of history that were ideological through and through. This close relationship between ideologies and conceptions of history should not surprise us. The nineteenth century was both the century of the rise of history as an academic discipline and that of the rise of modern political ideologies. History as a discipline developed within a climate that was variously progressive-liberal, revolutionary, conservative, reactionary, nationalistic, and radical. These political ideologies themselves contain views about history and its course. This holds true for all political and moral standards. The ecological, feminist, republican, postcolonial, and bio-political perspectives on the world that have developed in more recent times also contain (sometimes hidden) specific views on history and its course.

In White's analysis of nineteenth-century historians, ideologies also have a cognitive function. Conservatism enabled Ranke to view church and state in the nineteenth century as the results of an age-old process in which European nations had realized themselves. Anarchism enabled the French historian Jules Michelet (1798–1874) to view church and state as obstacles to the development of communities. Liberalism made Tocqueville emphasize having free choice in history. And the reactionary views of Nietzsche's friend Jacob Burckhardt made his time look pale in comparison with the sparse cultural highlights of the past, such as those of the Renaissance.

White also emphasizes the aesthetic nature of history-writing. But unlike Ankersmit, he does not focus on the artistic talent of the individual historian, but rather on the literary forms that the historian chooses to use. White argues that the realism of nineteenth-century historians essentially derives from poetic insights. Here, realism refers to the views that the historian has about the past and the nature of historical change. The historians he studies choose a certain form, *a mode of emplotment*, with which they present their respective histories. That choice is limited to the four plot types which are common to the Western tradition of storytelling and the nineteenth century: comedy, romance, tragedy, and satire. Does history evolve from a state of struggle to one of harmony, as the comedy prescribes? Did the church and state reach a state of harmony in Europe in the nineteenth century, after the struggle of the wars of religion in the seventeenth century, as Ranke believed? Or is the hero victorious in history, and with it the good and the just, as the romance teaches, as Michelet thought, who had found his hero in the French people? Or is it the fate of societies to turn against themselves, as the tragedy makes us believe, and as Tocqueville recounts in his histories? Or do the rare highlights of the past show that there is no progression, direction, or meaning to be found in the past, as the satire used by Burckhardt shows?

White concludes in his *Metahistory* that: 'the best grounds for choosing one perspective on history rather than another are ultimately aesthetic or moral rather than epistemological' (p. xii): aesthetic, because the historians' perspectives are essentially poetic insights; moral, because every perspective on history, every conception of history, is based on specific political-ideological views. Since no one form is more realistic than the other, and therefore does not represent reality more truthfully than the other, we have no basis for preferring one perspective over another on epistemological grounds.

For White, the realism of the historian coincides with the historian's perspective on history, with her conception of history; hence the title of his book. Every historian has views that are concerned with history itself, its course and meaning, and so every historian conceives of and develops a meta-history in order to write his or her history.

With the publication of *Metahistory*, the question whether history is a science or not once again made it to the agenda of the theory of history. In the 1970s it was believed that the answer to that question had already been given: History is a science insofar as it is a social science, as we discussed in the previous chapter. As a science, history as a discipline should keep its distance from literature, politics, and ideology. White argues the opposite. He proves to be the most widely read and discussed philosopher of history of the last 50 years. He would often point the historian to literature as an example, and as a result, many historians could not always identify with his work. According to them, the narrative they present is not a *literary artefact*, as White claims in one of the many essays he published before and after *Metahistory*, but a way of thinking, a cognitive instrument, as Ankersmit claims, to connect events and to see coherence in them.

White has more to teach about history-writing, its usefulness, and its disadvantages. His most important lesson will be discussed in Chapter 7. First, we will investigate why proper history takes the form of a narrative.

6. Narration

Living through a historical event is marked by not knowing how it will end. The resolution to an event first becomes known when the event itself is past and becomes the subject of stories told subsequently. As actors – in real life and as characters in a story – we do not have the omniscience of the narrator. The narrator's knowledge of how things turn out determines what events are recounted in what order. Such knowledge allows for a coherence that is typical of narrative, which in turn allows its readers and spectators to follow the story, as they anticipate how events unfold towards some conclusion.

There is a doubleness to action of which both history and poetics make us aware. The American philosopher Arthur Danto (1924–2013) puts it thus in his 1965 book *Analytical Philosophy of History*:

> It is a commonplace piece of poetic wisdom that we do not see ourselves as others do, that our image of ourselves is often signally different from the image held by others, that men constantly over- or under-estimate the quality of their accomplishments, their failures, and their dispositions.

Such wisdom is not only found in literature, theatre, and film but also, as Danto observes:

> These discrepancies [between our image of ourselves and the image held by others] are nowhere more marked than in history, where in the nature of the case we see a man's behaviour in the light of events future to his performances, and significant with respect to them. (p. 183)

When we think we are in control of our situation, and are confident about our choices and their outcome, history may show us otherwise and make evident both our lack of control and the extent of our self-deception, seen from the perspective of a later moment in time. History is the science of *unintended* consequences, as Ankersmit recently put it in an interview: A science of how decisions result in consequences one did not want and could not foresee.

One can still be an optimist and underline how the present is the result of choices for which humanity is fully responsible. And even though some consequences were unintended and unforeseen, in the end, things turned out for the better and progress was made. In this optimistic view of history, the discrepancy between the image we have of ourselves and the image held by others still holds, for no one knows in advance when or at what cost a better future will in fact be realized.

In the discrepancy between the image we have of ourselves and the image others have of us, the inevitability of progressing time and hence of history is experienced. Narrative allows us to deal with this discrepancy. It does so on a personal level, when we are the subjects of the stories we tell about our own lives, or when we recognize ourselves in the characters of a story, the dilemmas they face, and the obstacles they need to overcome. Historical narratives deal with this discrepancy on a collective level, where individuals are caught up in some social change which only becomes fully apparent in retrospect. This chapter deals with why proper history takes the form of narrative.

Historical Experience

The first recorded historical experience in what would become Western history is found in Homer's *Odyssey*. At some point in the story, Odysseus, on his voyage home after the Trojan War, arrives incognito at the court of the Phaeacians, where the bard Demodocus sings at the evening banquet about the actions and sufferings of the Greeks in the Trojan War. Suddenly, Odysseus's deeds and sufferings were put before him and he saw his own image through the eyes of the bard, which made him experience the discrepancy between past and present.

Such a historical experience also motivated Thucydides to write his history of the Peloponnesian War. The war was unintended and its unfolding unforeseen. Its principle actors even felt that is was inevitable. The Athenians believed that they had no choice but to maintain their empire, and the Spartans were certain that their fear for their own empire was justified. The war showed how people find themselves in situations they did not foresee and which they are unable to control: because of chance; because of disasters such as the plague in Athens; because fear, ambition, and self-interest take the upper hand and lead to wrong and short-sighted decisions; because of unrealistic views such as those held by the Melians; and because certain situations compel humans to do things they otherwise would not do. Even though actors believe in what they say and do, it often turns out that they are self-deceived.

A similar historical experience is found in the work of Italian humanists, most notably in the work of the Florentine aristocrat and statesman Guicciardini. As many of his contemporaries, he saw in hindsight how the French invasion of Italy in 1494 turned out to be an epochal event. The year was, as he writes in his *Storia d'Italia* (*History of Italy*),

> A most unhappy year for Italy, and in truth the beginning of those years of misfortune, because it opened the door to innumerable horrible calamities. (p. 32)

The events in the decades following the invasion revealed how chance affected the course of events, how such a course was uncontrollable, and how limited man's power was. The Italian states had not only fallen to the mercy of the European powers, causing the collapse of Italian independence, but also to the mercy of fortune and of imprudent princes.

The discrepancy between the actor's point of view and the narrator's point of view is a discrepancy between life and stories. The more profound the discrepancy is felt to be, the more historical awareness it generates.

Thucydides participated, as would Guicciardini nearly two millennia later, in the events he narrates and thus personally experienced the discrepancy between the actor's point of view and the narrator's point of view. He presents his account in what is at first sight a chronological order, following the sequence of events per season. But his knowledge of later events determines how earlier events are understood and henceforth described. The end of the war is already present in the beginning of the book. Thucydides is, after all, able to claim that it is the greatest war of all time in terms of the people who were affected by it and the suffering it caused. Although historians have to represent the events they relate accurately, which involves among other things stating their correct chronological order, they do not *understand* the past chronologically. Take Thucydides' description of the 427 civil war between democrats and oligarchs in Corcyra, a city on the island of present-day Corfu. He writes:

> So cruel was the course of this civil war [*stasis*], and it seemed all the more so because it was among the first of these. Afterwards, virtually all Greece was in upheaval, and quarrels arose everywhere between the democratic leaders, who sought to bring in the Athenians, and the oligarchs, who wanted to bring in the Spartans. (III.82)

What is of interest to us here is that at the moment of the civil war, it could not have been known that it was the first of a series of civil upheavals. The same holds true for Thucydides' comment that the civil war in other cities far exceeded the one in Corcyra in terms of the brutality of the attacks and its forms of revenge. Such knowledge of future events is only available to the narrator after the fact. Historical actors at best may anticipate or predict how events will unfold, but they cannot know how the events will in fact unfold.

Most academic historians and other scholars studying the past deal with a past which they did not personally live through. But the discrepancy between the point of view of the historical actors and their retrospective point of view is what defines their work as a historical narrative, for it allows the connection of later events to earlier events into one integrated whole, an ensemble of interrelated connections. This also makes it clear that the chronicle, which is typically a series of contemporary observations, does not provide us with a model for proper history (even if we admit that many chronicles do contain retrospective observations and are aspiring narratives). A chronicle misses the ending that is typical of narrative, and the coherence such an ending creates.

The Ideal Chronicler and Narrative Sentences

Historians easily move in time, going backwards and forwards in the years counted, relating later events to earlier events. Danto emphasizes in this context the use of words such as *the first, the last, anticipates, began, instigated, gave rise to, correctly predicted,* and *preceded*. These terms are commonly used in sentences that relate a later event to an earlier event. Danto calls these sentences *narrative sentences*. He writes:

> Their most general characteristic is that they refer to at least two time-separated events though they only *describe* (are only *about*) the earliest event to which they refer. (p. 143)

Consider Thucydides' statement that the civil strife in Corcyra was among the first of a series of such events. The sentence *refers* to the civil strife in Corcyra and to other civil conflicts later in time, but it is *about* the civil strife in Corcyra, for it asserts that this particular struggle is the first in a series. Or consider Guicciardini's statement that the French invasion of Italy in 1494 was the beginning of years of misfortune. It *refers* to the invasion and the events in the decades following it, but it is *about* the first event referred to, the French invasion, which, the statement asserts, was a beginning.

For a narrative sentence to be true, the events referred to need to have occurred, but its truth is also dependent on the later event(s) referred to. In 1483 there is nothing that would make the sentence 'The author of *Storia d'Italia* is born' true – just as in 427 there is no truth of the matter to the statement that the civil strife in Corcyra is among the first of a series. It follows, as Danto concludes, that verifiability is not an adequate criterion to determine the meaning of narrative sentences. Understanding a narrative sentence requires at a minimum the temporal distance that permits knowledge of the later event to which the earlier event is connected. Once again, the discrepancy between the image we have of ourselves and the image others have of us at a later moment in time is emphasized.

To further substantiate his argument on narrative sentences, Danto invokes something he calls 'the Ideal Chronicler'. He knows what happens the moment it happens, including what goes on within the minds of the historical actors. This Ideal Chronicler is in other words the perfect witness to events, knowing everything that is to be known about the event in question. But this Ideal Chronicler does not have knowledge of future events and how they are related to the events he registers in his chronicle. He is, in other words, and despite all his knowledge of the present, unable to make narrative sentences.

With this, Danto points at an important limitation in the concept of *verstehen*, the understanding of the minds of historical actors. Even a perfect witness to an event cannot provide historians with the knowledge they need, because that depends on the later events with which the event is connected. This is not, of course, to say that historians should not be interested in the beliefs, interests, and intentions of historical actors and their contemporaries, and how they saw the situation they were in. But such interest in the actor's point of view is not what history is about. Proper history takes the form of a narrative rather than a chronicle, even if the latter may seem more suited to represent reality as it appears. If we were to build a time machine, which for instance would enable us to wander around a pre-modern city exactly as it was, day by day, and record our observations, we would not be doing history, but we would be chronicling, registering what happens the moment it happens.

The narrative sentence also points to another insight into the nature of history: There is no definitive description of the past. This is so because new events will always allow us to re-describe past events. Danto concludes that all accounts of the past are therefore essentially incomplete. Although events obviously have a meaning for those who lived through them, the historical significance of past events is determined by their relation to later events, including future events, and since we have no knowledge of those future events, we can never provide a complete account of the past as long as the future remains unresolved. Even being able to predict future events by extrapolating them from current and past events and trends will not do, for, as Danto points out, to write a complete account of the past

> It will be necessary to know *which* future events are relevant, and this requires predicting the *interests* of future historians. (p. 169)

Any prediction as to the interests of future historians is nothing but idle speculation. It depends on the world they live in, and what is important to them in accordance with what has occurred. What future historians will say about our time therefore cannot be determined. The answer depends on what happens in the future, how those events affect what historians think is relevant, and how they connect those events to the events in our time.

Historical actors have no knowledge of the future. To be sure, historians lack such knowledge too, but they possess knowledge of the future of the past lives being studied, which the historical actor lacks. Now, obviously, narratives do not solely consist of narrative sentences. And many sentences in historical narratives describe the way things were in the eyes of the actors and their own contemporaries, including their desires, hopes, fears, and memories. It is important that the historian understands the way actors understood their world. A narrative sentence within a narrative is at best an indication that some event is significant for some reason. This is what Danto writes:

> A particular thing or occurrence acquires historical *significance* in virtue of its relation to some other thing or occurrence in which we happen to have some special interest, or to which we attach some importance, for whatever reason. Narrative sentences then are frequently used to justify the *mention*, in a narrative, of some thing or event whose significance might otherwise escape a reader. (p. 167)

Since it is the historian's interest or sense of importance that determines what event is significant and for what reason, it is therefore up to the historian to make history. This the historian does, as Danto claims, by relating later events to earlier events, and situating them into a temporal whole, a narrative, for an event or deed is significant only in the context of a story, that is, in connection to later events. Such is the advantage of hindsight, of seeing events and actions in temporal perspective.

Many historians do not tell stories with a clearly defined beginning initiating the story, a middle where some change – a reversal of fortune – takes place, and an ending which brings closure to the story. We should follow White and distinguish between

> a discourse that openly adopts a perspective that looks out on the world and reports it and a discourse that feigns to make the world speak itself and speak itself *as a story*. (p. 7)

In a story, events appear to tell themselves, and the reader or spectator follows the story from beginning to end. Incidentally, in case of a narrative of real events, such a beginning and ending are not the result of poetic ordering but of retroactively connecting later events to earlier events. In the case of a narrative that does not tell a story but rather presents the historian's perspective on the past, the historian self-consciously presents her view and the insight the work offers to her readers. The rationale of connecting later events to earlier events is that it allows the historian to answer the most important of historical questions: Why is this event historically significant?

Significance

It is up to the historian to determine the significance of an event, and this is done on the basis of later events, as well as on the basis of the historian's own interests and the question requiring answers, both of which are affected by those later events. Here, I want to make it clear that the conclusion or thesis reached by the historian is her determination of the historical significance of the event studied.

Evidently, questioning the significance of an event is different from asking what method or explanation is used. The historical *conclusion* or *thesis* should also be distinguished carefully from the *argument* the historian makes to support it. I will discuss three historical studies in support of this: one study we have discussed previously, a second which is also relevant to some of the topics discussed in this chapter, and a third which makes clear that it is the historian who decides how and why an event is historically significant. In short, the significance of an event does not repose in the event itself.

Recall Hunt's book *Politics, Culture, and Class in the French Revolution* which we discussed in the previous chapter. The investigation of the significance of the French Revolution leads to her historical thesis, namely that the revolution allowed for the invention of a new political culture, a revolutionary politics that brought ideology into being. This thesis she sees illustrated in a wide variety of cultural expressions, each of which retroactively exemplifies her conclusion. *Method* has to do with how the evidence is selected and studied, *theory* with what explains the existence of the evidence, and *argument* with how the evidence supports the claim that revolutionary politics inhibited the wide variety of cultural expression. But the historical *thesis* has to do with the historical significance of the Revolution, and specifically how it brought ideology into existence and thereby shaped our modern world. This thesis orders the events in the narrative in the sense that it makes the events lead up to this conclusion. This, Hunt is telling us, is how the Revolution should be seen. She concludes that the Revolution still intrigues us precisely because:

> It gave birth to so many essential characteristics of modern politics. [...] It was the moment in which politics was discovered as an enormously potent activity, as an agent for conscious change, as the mold for character, culture, and social relations. (p. 236)

This is the conclusion or insight she offers and also why the book is of value. Of course, to appreciate it fully we should read the book in its entirety, so that everything Hunt says about the Revolution is understood in terms of the perspective she offers.

Another example, which is also of interest for our understanding of some of the topics discussed in this chapter, comes from the political scientist J. Peter Euben (1939–2018). In his *The Tragedy of Political Theory*, published in 1990, Euben writes:

> The principal object of this book is to consider Greek tragedy insofar as it provides a preface for understanding classical political theory and to suggest that the tragedians and these theorists provide in turn a ground for contemporary theorizing. (p. 4)

This is how Greek tragedy is historically significant. As said, studying what makes something historically significant leads Euben to his historical thesis. This thesis is itself directly connected to the value of the book for our day, since Euben's goal for his book is to provide a 'point of reference and energy for understanding contemporary American culture' and 'invigorate our political and theoretical sensibilities'. (p. 304).

It obviously was not the intention of the tragedians Euben studies to provide a preface to the work of political theorists such as Thucydides and Plato, let alone to contemporary political theory. And even if the tragedians had intended to provide a ground for political thinking for all future to come, they would not have had any knowledge of that future or of how their work anticipated certain of our contemporary critiques (here Euben for example thinks of the critique that theory is reductionist). His argument is that tragedy 'helps constitute a democratic polity and challenges the democratic credentials of that polity'. (p. 18). The Athenians became a community through the theatre which made Greek plays, in contrast to our plays, TV broadcasts, and movies public events. Tragedians were, in short, civic educators. Euben:

> What the assembled citizenry witnessed was its past political choices, institutional forms, and cultural practices 'problematized' in the situations, themes, and characters on stage. (p. 51)

This allowed them to reflect on the human condition, on justice, and on the social order and its dangers, which in turn encouraged them to engage in political deliberation.

Euben distinguishes three issues in his reading of the selected authors: justice, identity (how one acts and speaks determines who one is), and the idea of membership in a political community. This is his method. Since the tragedians anticipated the political theorists, of whom Thucydides is one, it is not surprising that Euben emphasizes that Thucydides imitates the tragedians, in particular Euripides. Both tragedians and political theorists discuss the same themes:

> the simultaneity of justice and transgression, accomplishment and ruin, health and disease, insight and blindness, reason and tyranny that mark both Greek tragedy and political theory. (p. 34)

Euben mostly focuses on Thucydides' account of the civil strife in Corcyra which is, according to him, about 'what the absence of justice and the loss of identity means for individuals and cities' (p. 44). It marks the beginning of political theory in that political theory is itself a response to *stasis* ('political strife') and to the corruption and violence that accompany it.

There is evidence to support the argument that political theory is a response to civil war, which is the most extreme form of political disarray and social disintegration – the dismemberment of a community, as Euben puts it. There is evidence for the argument that tragedy in the fifth century B.C. provided the occasion in which the Athenians felt themselves to be members of a political community, given the central place of tragedy in the religious festivities of the city. There is also evidence to support the claim that Thucydides was influenced by the tragedians in terms of his subject matter and his book's structure. But the historical significance of both tragedy and Thucydides' account of the civil war in Corcyra for the time afterwards requires a historical thesis, which at the same time ensures the coherence of the narrative, making each event part of a temporal whole.

A third example, this time a microhistory written by the French historian Alain Corbin (*b.* 1936), illustrates how it is up to the historian to determine the historical significance of events. His 1990 *Le Village des Cannibales* is concerned with the brutal peasant murder of a nobleman during broad daylight in the French village of Hautefaye in 1870. His argument is that the peasants did not behave irrationally; the murder was a political and rational deed. There had been rumours at the time that the Prussian-led German army, which had invaded France a month earlier, was in the vicinity. This caused social anxiety among the peasants who were also hostile towards the nobility and the clergy (a sentiment dating back to the French Revolution), whom they believed were plotting to overthrow the beloved emperor. Their victim was a nobleman and, so they (mistakenly) believed, a Republican, which made him an enemy, a 'Prussian'. Corbin summarizes his argument thus:

> On August 16, 1870, the peasants on the fairground at Hautefaye were attempting to exorcise the fear that held them in its grips, attempting to ward off an imminent disaster. Dreadfully certain that their homes would be sacked and burned if the emperor fell victim to treason, they were quick to burn the 'Prussian' in their midst. (p. 83)

But why is this event, which appears insignificant in comparison to the Franco-Prussian War, historically significant?

The murder, Corbin tells us on the first page of his book, was the 'last outburst of peasant rage to result in murder'. This narrative sentence already hints at the thesis he proposes in his book. The contemporaries of the murder were horrified by the event, which conjured the ghost of peasant uprising which they had believed to have been laid to rest; but this event proved otherwise and they called the murderers monsters and cannibals. Their reaction, so Corbin concludes:

> Is a striking indication of how rapidly the average nine-teenth-century person had lost touch with the everyday violence of another era. It throws into sharp relief an anthropological transformation that had been under way since the first emergence of the *l'âme sensible*, the sensitive soul. (p. 119)

Here, Corbin finds the historical significance of the event. The reaction to the anachronistic murder, typical of an era believed to be long past, exemplifies the changing attitude towards violence and the rise of the sensitive soul, which still inhabits us to this day. Historical actors participate in and witness the changing world around them. But only from the point of view of the historian do events become historically significant, and does it become evident how the attitudes, beliefs, and behaviour of individuals exemplify changes in society.

The three examples discussed make it clear that evidence does not dictate what story is to be told. It is, after all, up to the historian to determine the significance of an event. This is not to deny that evidence *constrains* what can be said about the past. But the purpose of history is to provide insight into events for which there is evidence, to select and order those events (and the evidence for them), and to see coherence in them. None of these things is dictated by the evidence itself, but by the interests of the historian, by the questions she or he asks, and by the later events to which the earlier events are connected. These insights or perspectives function as a guide, telling us how the past is to be understood. In the previous chapter, we made it clear that we can rationally discuss these perspectives in terms of such criteria as scope, originality, consistency, and precision. And when we say that a narrative is *true*, we are saying that the perspective it offers is, at present, the best guide to the past that we have at hand.

These remarks might suggest that there are no impulses from the past that constitute a need for historical narration. There are, however, two such impulses. One is the historical experience we discussed earlier. The other has to do with the subject matter of genuine history.

The Subject of History

Narrative provides a way of dealing with the discrepancy between our own image of ourselves and the image others have of us at a later moment in time, when the outcome of what we did and lived through is known and things may have turned out differently than we expected. On a collective level and in the case of narratives of real events, this discrepancy is dealt with inasmuch as individuals are caught up in some kind of social change. All genuine history is concerned at some level with social change, that is, with a sociopolitical order in which individuals interact with one another in a context of norms and laws which they take to be theirs. Individuals appropriate these defining aspects of social life, including their recorded past appearances, which, to them as members of the community, explain (in the sense of making intelligible) how the community came to be what it is in the present. There is, in other words, a close relationship between narrative, history, and legislation, which is part of the moral character, the ethos, of a political community in a certain day and age. In this, White agrees with Hegel when he writes in his 1980 essay 'The Value of Narrativity':

> When [...] it is a matter of providing a *narrative* of real events, we must suppose that a subject of the sort that would provide the impulse to record its activities must exist. Hegel insists that the proper subject of such record is the state, but the state is to him an abstraction. The reality which lends itself to narrative representation is the conflict between desire, on the one side, and the law, on the other. (p. 16)

Human beings, Hegel emphasizes, have a desire for justice, morality, private property, freedom, social interaction, intercourse, and so on. To satisfy such desires, laws are to be enacted; individuals need to be both aware and capable of appropriating these laws as their own. According to Hegel, the latter circumstance is, for example, absent in India since the caste system prevents such appropriation; this explains to Hegel why the Indians of his own day, despite their many cultural achievements, did not have recorded history. In his *Vorlesungen über die Philosophie der Geschichte*, he tells us:

> First in the state with the awareness of laws there are clear actions available, and with them the clarity of awareness about them, which give the ability and the need to record them. (p. 115)

Now we can also understand Hegel's initially enigmatic remark that historical events and historical narration appeared simultaneously. A truly *historical* event is an action occurring in a sociopolitical order, which thereby produces an impulse for recording and narrating. Evidently, not all history-writing is the result of such an impulse. But a truly genuine history has as its subject a sociopolitical order, the ideals it needs to realize, and the conflicts, struggles, and obstacles it needs to overcome. All human beings, Hegel would add, have a desire for morality, justice, and freedom, a desire that requires a sociopolitical order, a state, to be fulfilled.

This is perhaps the most important insight of Hegel's social philosophy. An action in a sociopolitical order provides a need for historical narration because such narration enables self-understanding, allowing humans to reflect on their desire for justice and freedom. This will be the theme of our next chapter.

7.   The Historical Sublime

If you want to have a realistic view of the future, you need to study the past. Many will endorse this statement. For isn't the future an extension of the past? Doesn't the past tell us what is realistic, practical, and socially responsible, and for what reasons? And doesn't knowledge of the past prevent us from making the same mistakes over and over again? Just as knowledge of our own past enables us to make realistic plans for our own future, knowledge of our society's past is useful if we want to determine which direction that society is going and which way it should be heading.

The historicists would emphasize that every circumstance is different. Therefore, we cannot learn anything from the past. The more knowledge and insight we gain into the past, the better we are aware of this. But the historicists would also argue that the knowledge and insights that historians and other academics offer provide the only basis for determining which kind of politics is at present realistic, socially responsible, and practically feasible, even though historical knowledge and insights do not offer ready-made solutions to the problems at hand. How can we make decisions about the future without having historical knowledge of international relations, economic systems, institutions, migration, pandemics, social cohesion, emancipatory movements, dividing practices, and the rule of law, and how they each work?

It goes without saying that politicians are expected to have at least *some* historical knowledge of the social and political issues with which they are concerned. Therefore, the work of the historian has at least some influence on the politics pursued in the present. White refers to this influence as 'the politics of historical interpretation', in a 1982 essay by the same name. By this, he means the following:

> The politics *of* interpretation [...] has to do with the kind of *authority* the interpreter [e.g. the historian] claims vis-a-vis the established political authorities of his society, on the one side, and vis-a-vis other interpreters in his own field of study or investigation, on the other, as the basis of whatever *rights* he conceives himself to possess and whatever *duties* he feels obliged to discharge as a *professional* seeker of truth. (p. 113)

As an academic discipline, history brings the historian into existence. Historians derive their authority, and the rights and duties that come with it, from that discipline. They know how to do historical research. They know the history of history-writing – at least within their specific subfield – and have some sense of the theoretical problems the discipline faces. Historians are allowed to call themselves such when they have successfully completed their university education and have obtained the necessary degree. And they have a duty to be independent, reliable, verifiable, honest, and careful. The appeal to authority in choosing one historical interpretation over another is, according to White, a form of politics because it is a form of exercising influence and therefore power.

This politics of interpretation comes into play in the case of conflicting historical interpretations within the discipline. It also concerns the negligence of events, voices, and narratives in the past, which, for various reasons, are deemed a poor fit with the dominant interpretation. Think for example of Eurocentric conceptions of social and political events, and how they tend to discard those features of developments in the non-West that do not fit with their Western counterparts.

The politics of interpretation also plays a role when, in public debate, reference is made to the past to justify certain policies in the present. History is not only a story *about* power but also in its own right a form of *exerting* power. Ideally, historians take part in public debate directly, or indirectly when their work is consulted by the debate's participants. Historians may claim their authority and choose one historical interpretation over the other. Furthermore, when it comes to matters of fact, historians have a specific task. If facts are ignored, denied, invented, silenced, or distorted, historians must name and rectify those facts by pointing to evidence supporting them and by emphasizing that a certain question and method will lead to a particular selection of facts, each of which, if they are indeed facts and not fabrications, is irrefutable. Historians should also add that any selection of facts may mislead. But their most important task is to give those facts meaning by interpreting them. Facts don't speak for themselves.

In his essay, White has a specific form of the politics of historical interpretation in mind. He wants historical studies to support the awareness of the *dignity* and *freedom* of human existence. His thesis is that precisely that use of history has come under pressure in the modern (i.e., since the early nineteenth-century) understanding of history and the realism that is associated with history as a profession (which solidified in that century). Such is his criticism of the discipline. I will explain White's thesis in parts. In this chapter, we will think once again about the modern concept of history and its usefulness. It will discuss the historical sublime and its importance for our understanding of history.

Realism as Anti-Utopianism

White has no problems with the idea that knowledge of the past helps us to determine which decisions in the present are socially responsible, realistic, and practically feasible. He therefore wants politicians to be guided in their decisions by the realism inherent in history as a discipline, and the knowledge and insights it yields. He does not dispute that history is of use in that sense. In his essay, White is concerned with something else. He writes:

> The problem [...] lies with a conception of historical studies that purports to be above politics and at the same time rules out as 'unrealistic' any political program or thought in the least tinged with utopianism. And it does so, moreover, by so disciplining historical consciousness as to make realism effectively identical with anti-utopianism. (pp. 119–120)

The discipline, which aims to be above politics, brings us back to Ranke and the ideal that historians should erase themselves from their work, be impartial, abstain from praise and judgement, let the facts speak for themselves, and focus on *das reine Sehen der Dinge* (the pure vision of things). The exclusion of utopian political programmes as unrealistic takes us back to the historicist view that the present and the future are the products of the past and are therefore an extension of it. This means that a radical break with the present, as advocated in utopian and visionary politics, is unrealistic. The historical process moves in a certain direction and the knowledge of historical developments offers insights into that direction, or so the realists say.

The Russian-British philosopher and historian of ideas Isaiah Berlin (1909–1997) puts it thus: Utopias do not do justice to the historical facts; they ignore the wheels of history, the flow of time in which things rise, flourish, and fall. According to Berlin, utopian thinking has been disqualified since the nineteenth century on the basis of arguments such as these. In his essay, White is concerned with this influence, with this politics of historical interpretation, in which the realism of the historian is at the service of realism in political thinking, thereby dismissing utopian political programmes as unrealistic. He laments this effect of historical interpretation. It's a Nietzschean theme. Just as White would a century later, Nietzsche emphasized in his 1874 essay that historical thinking stands in the way of the formation of a challenging and original ideal:

> You have enough to ponder and invent by pondering that future life; but do not ask history to show the How? and Wherewith? [...] The historical sense, if it rules *without restraint* and unfolds all its implications, uproots the future because it destroys illusions. (p. 38)

White defines a visionary, utopian politics as a politics that puts the freedom and dignity of human existence first. According to him, as a discipline, history should support utopian thinking instead of disqualifying it as unrealistic. But how? This brings us to the heart of White's 1982 essay. His argument is that the appeal of utopian thinking can only be found in the contrast it offers with the 'historical sublime' as it has been described by the German philosopher, poet, playwright, and historian Friedrich von Schiller (1759–1805) in his 1801 essay *Über das Erhabene* (*On the Sublime*): as 'a "spectacle" of "confusion," "uncertainty" and "moral anarchy"' (p. 128). These sublime events are the horrors of the past which are incomprehensible and constitute the opposite of utopias; think of slavery, war, terror, tyranny, epidemics, and crimes.

How the sublime past then serves to support a radically different politics in which human dignity and freedom come first, is not something which White himself makes clear. I will address this gap first. Then I will return to White's essay and what he has to say about the rise of the modern concept of history in the nineteenth century.

The Sublimity of the Past

In his 1790 *Kritik der Urteilskraf,* Kant argues that the sublime is a specific experience within ourselves which is evoked by objects of chaos, uncontrollable disorder, and destruction. These objects are frightening, make us shudder, and appeal to our sense of self-preservation, even though we are not actually in danger (if we were in danger, we would try to flee). Here, Kant follows the Irish-British philosopher and politician Edmund Burke (1729–1797) who argues that the urge for self-preservation is the basis of the sublime experience, making it one of the strongest feelings we can have. The sublime is a feeling of awe, 'a delightful horror, a sort of tranquillity tinged with terror' (p. 123), he wrote in 1757. His definition of the sublime is quoted by Kant.

Schiller's view of the sublime is related to that of Kant in his aforementioned critique. Through Kant's critique, Schiller, too, makes use of Burke's definition of the sublime. But unlike Burke and Kant, he explicitly relates the sublime to the past. (In Burke and Kant, we only incidentally find a remark in which the sublime is related to the past: They connect the sublime primarily to overwhelming and awe-inspiring nature.) In his *Über das Erhabene*, Schiller writes the following. The sublime is:

> the terrifying and delightful spectacle of the all destructive and again creative and again destructive change, of [...] man who sees himself surrounded by fate, the unstoppable flight from happiness, the deluded security, the triumphant injustice and the losing innocence.

History offers us ample instances of sublime events. But how can fate, flight from happiness, deluded security, triumphant injustice, confusion, uncertainty, moral anarchy, the loss of innocence, and the spectacle of creative and destructive change, justify a radically different politics in which human dignity and freedom come first?

The essay *Über das Erhabene* brings us back to the distinction between the domain of nature and necessity on the one hand, and the domain of reason and freedom on the other, which we discussed in Chapter 4 of this book. Following Kant, Schiller makes a distinction between man as a natural, sensory being and man as a rational, moral being. The sublime, he argues, makes jarringly clear that:

> the laws of nature are not necessarily ours too, and that we have an autonomous, first principle in ourselves that is independent of all sensory impressions.

The realization that we have a first principle in ourselves gives us our sense of dignity. Kant also emphasizes in his critique that the sublime reveals the ability to regard ourselves as independent from nature. The sense of self-preservation that the sublime relies on is the self-preservation of the human in us, he states. In this way the sublime makes us realize our autonomy and dignity as human beings. Schiller elaborates on this idea. He distinguishes the sublime from the beautiful (aesthetics), as Burke and Kant did before him, and adds the following: The sublime offers a way out of the sensory world while the beautiful would like to 'keep us imprisoned there forever'. This is Schiller's most important insight. He writes:

> With the beautiful, mind [*Vernunft*] and sensation are in harmony, and only because of this harmony does it appeal to us.

Think of a nice piece of music in reaction to which what one hears (sensory perception) and thinks of it (mind) are in harmony. Or think of seeing a beautiful painting or the beauty of nature, smelling the scent of a fragrant flower, touching a tree's bark, or tasting the sweetness of fresh fruit. These things are beautiful insofar as the sensory experiences and the mind are in harmony with each other.

> With the sublime, on the other hand, mind [*Vernunf*] and sensation do *not* harmonize with each other, and it is precisely in the conflict between these two wherein lies its wonder, with which it moves our state of mind [*Gemüt*]. Here physical and moral man are separated most sharply from one another.

This is how the sublime has a moral effect, and why White relies on Schiller to make his point. We know that the sublime spectacle is terrifying and makes us shiver, but instead of relying on our natural, sensory self when confronted with it, for example by fleeing or turning our heads, we rely on our non-physical selves, on our minds, through which we become aware of our independence from our sensory impressions, of our moral selves, and of our desire for dignity and freedom.

When we ask ourselves why history is relevant, we must not lose sight of the historical sublime. Because it is precisely the sublime spectacle that makes us realize that we are autonomous, moral beings, as Schiller argues. And as such the sublime is able to place the desire for human dignity and freedom at the centre of our understanding of the past. For that reason, Schiller's essay is important to White. The historian must present in his or her work the disorder, chaos, moral anarchy, uncertainty, and blind randomness of human existence in such a way that the readers or listeners become aware that they have within themselves a first principle, a desire to be free and have dignity. In this way the historical sublime can justify a radically different, utopian politics: One that puts human dignity and freedom first. With this White can also defend himself against those who would argue, against him, that utopias in the 20th century have primarily been associated with totalitarian regimes under which the dignity and freedom of man were stripped away and subordinated to the interests of the state (this association is also often made in science fiction).

In his 1982 essay, White presents a controversial example of what he has in mind. He states that the politics of the state of Israel from its foundation on is a moral response to the sublime history of the Jewish Diaspora. This shows the Israeli pursuit of dignity and freedom, despite the fact that it comes at the expense of the Palestinians – which is why White rejects that politics. The historical sublime does not justify that politics; it *does* justify the pursuit of dignity and freedom. According to him, the Palestinians should, in their pursuit of dignity and freedom, come up with a utopian ideal for themselves, in contrast to those parts of their past that are sublime. Only then does their existence acquire a meaning for which they alone are responsible.

The Historical Sublime and the Modern Concept of History

The historical sublime brings White back to the moment that history became a professional discipline in the nineteenth century. Before the nineteenth century, White argues, history was a 'spectacle of crimes, superstitions, errors, duplicities, and terrorisms'. (p. 129) This made it possible to justify a new kind of politics that would bring about a different and better future. White thinks, among other things, of the historical work of eighteenth-century Enlightenment philosophers and how they contributed to progressive politics, and of Schiller's own romantic-historical work.

In the nineteenth century, however, the notion of the sublime was driven out of any understanding of the historical process, according to White. He states:

> Historical facts are politically domesticated precisely insofar as they are effectively removed from displaying any aspect of the sublime that Schiller attributed to them. That is, insofar as historical events and processes become understandable, as conservatives maintain, or explainable, as radicals believe them to be, they can never serve as a basis for a visionary politics more concerned to endow social life with meaning than with beauty. (p. 128)

White presumably takes conservatives to be the historicist historians and philosophers who aim to understand events and processes from the motives and ideas underlying them. Events, from this perspective, contribute to the realization of the state or freedom over time. He presumably understands radicals to be those historians who take themselves to be social scientists who aim to explain behaviour and processes on the basis of social circumstances that determine social stratification and the possible discontent with it. With beauty, White refers to an aesthetic approach to historical research which he associates with the Rankeans. In their view, everything in the past that appears to be 'confusing' is a mere surface phenomenon:

> A product of lacunae in the documentary sources, of mistakes in ordering the archives, or of previous inattention or scholarly errors. (p. 127)

The desire to offer an explanation for what is confusing or to understand it means that order or coherence could still be found in the past. It

> permits the historian to see some beauty, if not good, in everything human and to assume an Olympian calm in the face of any current social situation, however terrifying it may appear to anyone who lacks historical perspective. (p. 127)

White locates the beginning of this 'desublimation' in the work of the aforementioned Burke on the French Revolution.

> Burke's *Reflections on the Revolution in France* can be seen as one of many efforts to exorcise the notion of the sublime from any apprehension of the historical process, so that the 'beauty' of its 'proper' development, which for him was given in the

example of the 'English constitution,' could be adequately comprehended. (p. 125)

By conceiving events as a component in the processes of change, and by assuming a 'proper' development of those processes of change, there is no room for a historical sublime to be understood or explained that is not part of such a process but stands on its own.

The latter becomes clearest in Hegel's philosophy of history. Hegel explicitly deals with this in his *Vorlesungen über die Philosophie der Geschichte*:

> But also when we see history as this slaughter-bench, on which the happiness of peoples, the wisdom of states and the virtue of individuals have been sacrificed, the question that is nevertheless raised is for what, to which end this inconceivable sacrifice has been made. (p. 64)

Given the catastrophes of the 20th century, inconceivable for Hegel at the time, the question 'to which end this inconceivable sacrifice has been made' no longer arises. But here the point is that the idea that the course of events manifests a certain direction or purpose leaves no room for the historical sublime. To have room for the historical sublime is to have a view of the past in which there is no meaning or principle to be discovered in or behind the course of events, no injustice that, in the end, serves some greater good.

The conclusion is not that the historian merely needs to display the sublime. If, for example, motives and intentions played a role in what would ultimately be sublime, then the historian should be attentive to that. But such is not to make the sublime understandable and part of a certain development.

History and Tragedy: Learning from Suffering

The meaninglessness of the past brings us back to the pessimism of Thucydides, Guicciardini, Burckhardt, and Nietzsche, and the idea that, as Guicciardini put it, perfection may be possible at the beginning, but all things human inevitably become corrupted in the course of time. Such is the human condition. Pessimists would emphasize how human choices have unintended consequences, and how rare it is to find politicians who make decisions for the benefit of all. Optimists, by contrast, would hold that there is progress and perfection at the end, when obstacles are overcome, even if such end is not a defined endpoint in time, but an 'infinite end' that man should strive to reach and realize again and again – think of such infinite ends as justice, freedom, and human dignity. The present is at least in part the product of human choices, and therefore, the future is too, which gives us the responsibility to take matters into our own hands.

The past, pessimists hold, has no inherent meaning: There is no plan, principle, or purpose in history, no deeper and underlying reason why things are the way they are, and no direction in which history is heading. Is science, Nietzsche asks himself rhetorically in the preface of the reprint of his *Die Geburt der Tragödie* (*The Birth of Tragedy*), not an escape from pessimism in its aim to replace art as the explainer of life? White essentially asks the same question: Isn't history, as an academic discipline, as it developed in the nineteenth century, a flight from the sublime spectacle offered by the past? Injustice, chaos, suffering, confusion, the inescapability of fate – all are part of human existence, without a deeper reason or justification for their presence in our lives. According to Nietzsche, this also means that the goal of humanity, and therefore of history, can never be found in its end, as Hegel suggests, but only in its best examples, as we saw in the first chapter of this book.

Nietzsche found the idea of pessimism among the Greeks in their desire for and impulse towards:

> tragic myth, towards images of all that is frightening, evil, puzzling, destructive, [and] fatal in human existence. (p. 10)

Only an aesthetic justification of existence can be given, according to Nietzsche. To him, the desire for beauty – the tragic arts – was born out of necessity, as a way to make the hardship of life tolerable. That is why tragedy generates a sublime experience through the depiction of what is 'frightening, evil, puzzling, destructive, [and] fatal in human existence'. It reminds us of Schiller and his views on the sublime and the beautiful (in his *Über das Erhabene* and his *Über die ästhetische Erziehung des Menschen*). For Schiller, both history and the tragic arts offer a view of the sublime, of (to quote the passage once more):

> the terrifying and delightful spectacle of the all destructive and again creative and again destructive change, of [...] man who sees himself surrounded by fate, the unstoppable flight from happiness, the deluded security, the triumphant injustice and the losing innocence.

This shows the strong affinity between the views of Schiller and those of Nietzsche. Nietzsche himself points this out in passing in his *Vom Nutzen und Nachteil der Historie*, when he remarks that historians tend to destroy the historical sublime – a remark White would repeat a century later.

Nietzsche quotes Schiller, who writes about the historian that:

> one appearance after the other begins to withdraw from blind approximation, from lawless freedom, and as a fit member joins the ranks of a coherent whole – *which, of course, only exists in his imagination.* (p. 35)

The coherent whole is made by the historian. It is the order and connections he sees, the developments he discerns in the manifold of events – a whole which did not exist, and could not have existed, for the people in the past themselves. For them there was only the reality of the moment, and the fear, hope, confidence, or steadfastness with which it was met.

In quoting Schiller, Nietzsche also once more underlines the importance of the subjectivity of the historian (a topic we discussed in Chapter 5). For us, the relationship with the views of White is of importance here. The sublime – sheer arbitrariness, the volatility of chaos – is erased from the understanding of the past, and therefore from history, because it does not fit into some orderly, coherent, and aesthetically pleasing historical development. In the nineteenth century, White says, the sublime became part of aesthetics instead of being distinguished from it.

These comments on Schiller and Nietzsche also make it clear that tragedy and history-writing are interconnected through the sublime spectacle, insofar as both represent what is 'frightening, evil, puzzling, destructive, [and] fatal in human existence'. This is an important observation. Over the last few decades, scholars have often pointed out that history and poetics are similar in form, often with reference to the work of White. The narrative form with which historians present events in a coherent way is said to have been derived from fiction. From this it was inferred that the boundary between fact and fiction is permeable, or even that history *is* a form of fiction. These scholars not only ignored the way in which the distinction between fact and fiction in thinking about historical studies has traditionally been thematized, but also discarded the shared origin of tragedy and historical study in the temporality, hardness, and uncertainty of human existence, and how tragedy (literature) and history, each in its own way, are responses to that. This is an old theme and it reminds us of Polybius and his statement that history is the teacher of life, with which we started the first chapter of this book. The only way man can bear the vicissitudes of life with dignity, he tells us, is to be reminded of the suffering of others.

The German philosopher Hans-Georg Gadamer (1900–2002) also points to the commonality of history and tragedy. He writes that the tragic poet Aeschylus (c. 525–456) was the first to emphasize that we learn by suffering. What we learn is that human existence is irreversible and finite, and there-fore has a limit that cannot be transcended. This insight is offered in both tragedy and in history-writing. According to Gadamer, it characterizes the historicity (*Geschichtlichkeit*) of every experience, and with that acknowledges that the finitude of existence is the basis of all historical thought. He puts it thus in his 1960 magnum opus *Wahrheit und Methode* (*Truth and Method*):

A genuine [*eigentliche*] experience is one in which man becomes aware of his finiteness. In it are found the limits of what can be done and the self-consciousness of his planning reason. It becomes clear that it is a mere illusion that every-thing can be reversed, that there is always time for everything and everything somehow returns. The one standing and acting in history rather experiences constantly that nothing returns. To acknowledge that which is, here does not mean: acknowledging that which exists only once, but [...] the insight that all expectation and planning of finite beings is finite and limited. Genuine experience is consequently the experience of one's own historicity. (p. 363)

To acknowledge the finiteness of existence, of existing within finite, irreversible time, is to possess historical consciousness. Or, as we put it in the previous chapter, the experience of the discrepancy between our contemporaneous image of ourselves and the image we have at a later moment in time, is a *historical* experience.

We learn of the irreversibility and finitude of our existence through suffering, Aeschylus teaches us. History as a discipline, therefore, cannot ignore the sublime, despite its nineteenth-century desire to drive the sublime out of the understanding of the past. The sublime makes us preeminently aware of the finiteness of existence. It throws us back onto ourselves, as Schiller states, making us realize that we have a first principle in ourselves, in that we find our desire for dignity and freedom. And then we can give existence a meaning for which only we are responsible. This is the important reason why attention must be paid to the sublime spectacle in history-writing. Once again it becomes clear that the answers to what history *is* and what its *use* is are mutually dependent.

We now have a better understanding of the shared origin of history and tragedy. The distinction between fact and fiction, between history and tragedy, has remained untouched. Historians do not invent and exaggerate. Their first task is to focus on what has been done within the finite existence of man.

Catharsis

I end this chapter with one more observation on the shared
origin of history and tragedy. I think Hannah Arendt was
right in her essay 'The Modern Concept of History', when she
stated that both history and tragedy are ultimately about:

> the 'reconciliation with reality,' the *katharsis*, which, according
> to Aristotle, was the essence of tragedy, and, according to
> Hegel, was the ultimate purpose of history. (p. 574)

Schiller and Nietzsche would, given what we said, agree
with Arendt in this regard. The suffering of others evokes
pity, which cleanses us inasmuch as it throws us back upon
ourselves, and helps us to accept existence and the world
we live in as they are.

To Hegel, reconciliation as the ultimate purpose of history
meant that his own philosophical history is a theodicy, a
justification of God,

> in that the evil in the world is understood, and the thinking
> spirit [*denkende Geist*] is reconciled with evil. (p. 56)

Understanding evil is vital to human self-understanding, to
the spirit comprehending itself. Arendt would have thought
of 20th-century totalitarianism, the rise of which was the
most important event of her lifetime. Stalin's Russia and
Germany's Nazism stood for evil itself, and totalitarianism
posed the greatest threat to a free and open society. Understanding totalitarianism was urgent for Arendt, and many
with her, for only such an understanding would allow the
reconciliation with the world, the coming to terms with it.
How are human beings capable of doing things that no one

thought possible beforehand? And which are, afterwards, only conceivable *because* they have taken place? A true historical event can neither be foreseen nor prevented. It is irrevocable and creates its own history, says Arendt. We reason backwards from the event, looking for its origin in its past and an answer to the question: How could this have happened? How, in short, are human beings capable of evil?

The idea that the reconciliation with social and political reality is the ultimate purpose of history brings us back to White's criticism of Hegel. Is reconciliation not aimed at answering the question to what end the sacrifices in the past have been made, an attempt to give the 'sin and suffering' of the past a meaning by locating it in some process or development? There is, however, more to Hegel's view than White seems to admit. For Schiller, and thus also for White, freedom and dignity are *intrinsic* to being human. Hegel, by contrast, maintains that freedom and dignity develop in history as part of the development of the spirit. The historical sublime, Hegel might admit, is indeed not part of some process that needs to be understood or explained. But the desire for freedom and dignity, of which the sublime makes us aware, does partake in the development of the spirit – of human social self-awareness – and the institutions in which this self-awareness is historically realized, such as, for example, the Universal Declaration of Human Rights and the International Court of Justice.

We are not to make the sublime understandable and part of a certain development. But the question for the Hegelians is, however, whether progress with regard to the realization of freedom and dignity has in fact been made in history, despite the catastrophes of the 20th century. For, as the German philosopher Theodor Adorno (1903–1969) contends: 'Auschwitz [...] makes all talk of progress towards freedom seem ludicrous.'

8.   Epilogue

In his 1966 essay 'The Burden of History', White writes in his uncompromising style:

> Anyone who studies the past 'as an end in itself' must appear as either an antiquarian, fleeing from the problems of the present into a purely personal past, or a kind of cultural necrophile, that is, one who finds in the dead and dying a value he can never find in the living. The contemporary historian has to establish the value of the study of the past, not as 'an end in itself', but as a way of providing perspectives on the present that contribute to the solution of problems peculiar to our own time. (p. 125)

Not being able to relate to the interests and problems of their time was the burden of the historian in the 1960s, and arguably, this burden still persists today. This burden can be lifted not only by offering helpful perspectives on the present but also by making us aware of the extent to which our present condition is the result of past choices, which means that the future, too, is our responsibility.

Recently, the American historians Jo Guldi (*b.* 1978) and David Armitage (*b.* 1965) offered a similar message in their 2014 book *The History Manifesto*. History, they argue, is a critical human science, and the arbiter of the future visions of societies, because it teaches about destiny and free will, about contingency and the openness of social processes; because it debunks myths and enables the critical assessment of economic and other indicators; and because it allows us to imagine alternatives to the social and political order in which we happen to live. All of these lessons are vital given present-day economic inequality, climate change, pandemics, globalization, and the role of big data in society. In their manifesto, Guldi and Armitage aim to resurrect the old view that history is the teacher of life.

Not everyone will agree with their manifesto. One objection readily presents itself: The historian is primarily interested in the past, not the present, as they suggest. But even those historians who underline the love for the past for its own sake, who emphasize that the past is different from the present, and who defend the interest in history as an end in itself, at some point believe that history is useful. If only because the study of the past makes us not merely smart for the moment (*klug für ein andermal*) but wise forever (*weise für immer*), as Burckhardt once said.

The usefulness of history as a discipline is usually understood in terms of the usefulness of the discipline for the present. History offers perspectives on the present in order to deal with the problems of its time. It provides insights into the past that help us orient ourselves in the present. We need history, it is said, to understand the present. As a subject in school, history is usually considered relevant for this very reason. Everyone should know how the society in which they live came about, what is specific (*eigen*) to it, and what events and people from that history have been decisive. The historian thus has a certain responsibility for the living. But the historian also has a certain responsibility for the past, for the dead.

According to the German philosopher and cultural critic Walter Benjamin (1892–1940), the living have a weak 'messianic' power to rectify past injustices in the present. Previous generations expect future generations to be relieved of the injustices inflicted upon them. History is not just for those who live now. Historians also write their history in the name of the dead and for the dead. Here, Benjamin is

Figure 6. *Angelus Novus*. Artist: Paul Klee, 1920. Benjamin bought this drawing in 1921 and saw in it the 'angel of history', who 'sees one single catastrophe which keeps piling wreckage upon wreckage'.

concerned with the victims of injustices, not with people from the past whom we now admire for their achievements, and whom we might like to be our ancestors. Where one sees progress in the past, or highlights, or a coherence of which success is its hallmark, others see, as Benjamin puts it, 'one single catastrophe which keeps piling wreckage upon wreckage'. (p. 249).

Benjamin's weak messianic power reminds us of Michelet and his view that historians should speak for the dead who grieve in their dreams for the circumstances in which they had to live their lives. The dead not only need the tears of the historian; their fate need not only be lamented, says Michelet. What they need is:

> an Oedipus who will solve for them their own riddle, which made no sense to them, one who will explain to them the meaning of their words, their own actions which they did not understand. (p. 158)

Michelet emphasizes that the historian must also make the silences in the past, the voices that were never heard, heard. Only when the voice of the dead and what could not or was not allowed to be said is heard, even if only once, may the dead find peace in their graves. Thus, history serves the dead and does justice to their lives.

In this, it is again apparent that what history is and what its value is are intertwined. This short book began with Nietzsche's statement that history should serve life. We have ended with the statement that history must also be at the service of the dead.

There is not one answer to what history is. There also is not one answer to what its use is. One conclusion is, however, warranted. Our linear, human, earthly existence is temporary, singular, perishable, and finite. That is why we look back and dwell on it. To do it justice. To condemn it. To understand it. To become wiser. To reconcile ourselves with it. For the inspiration and conciliation it offers. For the confidence it gives. And in order to realize it.

Sources and Notes

Chapter 1

The quotations are from Nietzsche, *On the Advantage and Disadvantage of History for Life*, translated by Peter Preuss, Indianapolis and Cambridge, 1980 [1874]. Nietzsche's preference for monumental history is evident from his 1873 *Die Philosophie im tragischen Zeitalter der Griechen*. In his 1889 *Götzen-Dämmerung oder Wie man mit dem Hammer philosophiert*, Nietzsche writes in the section 'Was ich den Alten verdanke' ('What I Owe the Ancients') that he feels most closely related to Thucydides. Cicero would canonize history's function as a teacher of life (*historia magistra vitae*). Earlier, Polybius had observed that this is claimed by all historians. See Polybius, *The Rise of the Roman Empire*, translated by Ian Scott-Kilvert, London, 1979, I.1. The views of Cicero on the use of history for the orator can be found in John Marincola, translation and introduction, *On Writing History, From Herodotus to Herodian*, London, 2017. The view that history is philosophical instruction with examples is sometimes attributed to the orator Dionysius of Halicarnassus (60 B.C.–7 A.D.), but it is not his: It is found in the work of an unknown author, which was preserved within Dionysius's own work. Niebuhr makes his comment on Roman history in the introduction of his *Römische Geschichte. Volume 1*, Cambridge, 2010 [1811]. For Barante, see his essay 'De l'Histoire' in: *Etudes historiques et biographiques*, Paris, 1857, volume 2.

Chapter 2

The quotations are from Thucydides, *On Justice, Power, and Human Nature: The Essence of Thucydides' History of the Peloponnesian War*, edited and translated by Paul Woodruff, Indianapolis and Cambridge, 1993. I prefer this translation above others. For Lucian's essay, see John Marincola, *On Writing History, From Herodotus to Herodian*. This volume contains many Greek and Roman views on history. The Arendt article to which I refer: 'The Modern Concept of History,' *The Review of Politics*, 20:4, 1958, pp. 570–590. An expanded version of it appears in Arendt, *Between Past and Future: Six Exercises in Political Thought*, Cleveland and New York, 1963, pp. 41–90. It is from this version that the quotation on Augustine is taken. Augustine criticizes the idea of continual renewal and repetition and the cyclical view of the world's history in Book XII of his *Concerning the City of God. Against the Pagans*, translated by Henry Bettenson and introduction by John O'Meara, Harmondsworth and New York, 1984. For 'national' Roman history, see the essay 'Fabius Pictor and the Origins of National History' by Arnaldo Momigliano in his *The Classical Foundations of Modern Historiography*, Berkeley and Los Angeles, 1990. Niebuhr speaks about Thucydides and Ephorus in his *Vorträge über alte Geschichte. An der Universität zu Bonn gehalten*, Erster Band, Berlin, 1847. Ranke's admiration for Thucydides is for example evident from his *Weltgeschichte*, Erster Band, München and Leipzig, 1921 [1881]. For organic nature as a model for conceptualizing societies, see for example Ranke's 1836 inaugural address, 'On the Relation of and Distinction between History and Politics,' in: Ranke, *The Theory and Practice of History*, edited and introduced by Georg G. Iggers, London and New York, 2011. Rather well known is the statement by Herder, 'was ich bin, bin ich geworden. Wie ein Baum bin ich gewachsen; der Keim war da; aber Luft, Erde und alle Elemente, die ich um mich setze, mussten beitragen, den Keim, die Frucht, den Baum zu bilden.' ('What I am, I have become. Like a tree I have grown; the seedling was there; but air, earth and all elements, that I gathered around me, had to contribute, for the seedling, the fruit, and the tree to grow.') J.G. Herder, *Vom Erkennen und Empfinden der menschlichen Seele*, in: B. Suphan, C. Redlich, *Sämtliche Werke. 33 Bände. Band VIII*, Berlin, 1877, p. 307. For Hegel's views on history, see his *Vorlesungen über die Philosophie der Geschichte*, Stuttgart, 2002. On p. 59, he makes a statement similar to Herder's. For the concept of the nation, see Guido Zernatto and Alfonso G. Mistretta, 'Nation: The History of a Word,' *The Review of Politics*, 6:3, 1944, pp. 351–366.

Chapter 3

The remarks by Savigny (respectively, p. 214 and p. 220) and Niebuhr's letters can be found in *The Life and Letters of Barthold George Niebuhr: With Essays on His Character and Influence*, Bunsen, Brandts, and Lorbell, New York 1854 [1838]. References are made to Humboldt, *Über die Aufgabe des Geschichtsschreibers*, 1821, in *Humboldt's gesammelte Werke*, Berlin 1841, pp. 1–25; Niebuhr, *Vorträge über römische Alterthümer. An der Universität zu Bonn gehalten*, Berlin, 1858; Herder, *Auch eine Philosophie der Geschichte zur Bildung der Menschheit*, Stuttgart, 1990 [1774]; Hegel, *Vorlesungen über die Philosophie der Geschichte*, Stuttgart, 2002. These lectures held in the 1820s have been published posthumously; Hegel, *Grundlinien der Philosophie des Rechts*, Berlin, 1821. See § 247–248 for his comments on colonialism; Niebuhr, *Römische Geschichte*.

Erster Theil, Berlin, 1811; Ranke, *Geschichten der Romanischen und Germanischen Völker von 1494 bis 1514*, third edition, Leipzig, 1884 [1824]; Grafton, *The Footnote: A Curious History*, Cambridge MA, 1997; Humboldt, *Über die innere und äussere Organisation der höheren wissenschaftlichen Anstalten in Berlin*, 1809/1810, http://edoc.hu-berlin.de/18452/5305; Ranke, *Sammtliche Werke, vol. 24*, Leipzig, 1872, for his inaugural address; Ranke, *The Theory and Practice of History*, edited and introduction by Georg G. Iggers, London and New York, 2011; and Windelband, *Geschichte und Naturwissenschaft. Rede beim Stiftungsfest der Kaiser Wilhelms Universität Strassburg am 1. Mai 1894*, Strassburg, 1894. Joachim Ritter argues that Hegel's philosophy is a philosophy of the French Revolution in his *Hegel and the French Revolution: Essays on the Philosophy of Right*, translation and introduction by Richard Dien Winfield, Cambridge MA and London, 1984 [1969]. For the Eurocentrism of historicism, see Edward Said, 'Orientalism Reconsidered,' *Cultural Critique*, 1:85, pp. 89–107. For Hegel on the Haitian Revolution, see Susan Buck-Morss, 'Hegel and Haiti,' *Critical Inquiry*, 26:4, 2000, pp. 821–865.

Chapter 4

References are to Hempel, 'The Function of General Laws in History,' *The Journal of Philosophy*, 39:2, 1942, pp. 35–48; Kant, *Groundwork for the Metaphysics of Morals*, edited and translated by Allen W. Wood, New Haven and London, 2002 [1785]; Hegel, *Vorlesungen über die Philosophie der Geschichte*, the quotation on freedom can be found on p. 59; Worster, *Dust Bowl: The Southern Plains in the 1930s*, Oxford, 2004 [1979]; Collingwood, *The Idea of History*, Oxford, 1978 [1946]; Scott, 'The Evidence of Experience,' *Critical Inquiry*, 17:4, 1991, pp. 773–797; and Ankersmit, *Narrative Logic: A Semantic Analysis of the Historian's Language*, Meppel, 1981. In the Netherlands, all dissertations are published in book form. A somewhat revised edition of his book was published in 1983. Scott is influenced by the work of the French historian and philosopher Michel Foucault (1926–1984). See his essay 'The Subject and Power,' *Critical Inquiry*, 8:4, 1982, pp. 777–795, for the different ways that subjects are made, and the idea of power as a subject acting upon another subject. The first mention of the model of explanation proposed by Hempel I know of is found in Windelband's rectorial address *Geschichte und Naturwissenschaft* (see notes to previous chapter). Like Hempel, Windelband emphasizes in this context the dispositional explanation of behaviour.

Chapter 5

References are to Ankersmit, 'In Praise of Subjectivity,' in: *Historical Representation*, Stanford, 2001, pp. 75–103; Scott, *Gender and the Politics of History*, revised edition, New York, 1999; Ankersmit, *Aesthetic Politics: Political Philosophy Beyond Fact and Value*, Stanford, 1996; Nietzsche, *On the Advantage and Disadvantage of History for Life*; Hunt, *Politics, Culture, and Class in the French Revolution*, Berkeley, 1984; and White, *Metahistory: The Historical Imagination in Nineteenth-Century Europe*, Baltimore and London, 1973.

Chapter 6

In this chapter, I make use of Arthur Danto, *Narration and Knowledge*, New York, 1985. This book includes the integral text of the revised edition of his 1965 *Analytical Philosophy of History*. The book-length interview with Ankersmit is by Leonie Wolters, *De Erfenis is op. De woorden van Frank Ankersmit*, Leusden, 2018. I furthermore made use of Thucydides, *The Peloponnesian War*; Guicciardini, *History of Italy*, translated by Sidney Alexander, Princeton, 1984 [1969]; White, 'The Value of Narrativity in the Representation of Reality,' *Critical Inquiry*, 7:1, 1980, pp. 5–27; my *The Exemplifying Past: A Philosophy of History*, Amsterdam, 2018; Hunt, *Politics, Culture, and Class in the French Revolution*; Euben, *The Tragedy of Political Theory. The Road not Taken*, Princeton, 1990; Corbin, *The Village of Cannibals: Rage and Murder in France*, 1870, translated by Arthur Goldhammer, Cambridge MA, 1992 [1990]; and Hegel, *Vorlesungen über die Philosophie der Geschichte*. Hegel is more specific about the desire for justice and freedom in his 1821 *Grundlinien der Philosophie des Rechts*.

Chapter 7

References are to White, 'The Politics of Historical Interpretation: Discipline and De-Sublimation,' *Critical Inquiry*, 9:1, 1982, pp. 113–137; Berlin, 'The Concept of Scientific History,' *History and Theory*, 1960, reprinted in Berlin, *Concepts and Categories: Philosophical Essays*, London, 1999 [1978], pp. 103–142; Burke, *A Philosophical Enquiry into the Origin of our Ideas of the Sublime and Beautiful*, edited and introduction by Adam Philips, Oxford, 1990 [1757]; Kant, *Kritiek van het oordeelsvermogen*, translated by Jabik Beenbaas and Willem Visser, Amsterdam, 2009 [1790], book 2, § 23–30 (Kant quotes Burke on p. 171); Hegel, *Vorlesungen über die Philosophie der Geschichte*;

Nietzsche, *Die Geburt der Tragödie* [1886], in: Nietzsche, *Werke in drie Bänden*, Volume 1, Cologne, 1994; Nietzsche, *On the Advantage and Disadvantage of History for Life*; Polybius, *The Rise of the Roman Empire*; Schiller, *Über das Erhabene*, in: *Schillers Sämmtliche Werke, vierter Band*, Stuttgart, 1879, pp. 726–738 (the online version of the text I used can be found at: https://gutenberg.spiegel.de/buch/ueber-das-erhabene-3301/1); Gadamer, *Wahrheit und Methode. Grundzüge einder philosophischen Hermeneutik*, Tübingen, 1990 [1960]; Arendt, 'The Modern Concept of History,' *The Review of Politics*, 20:4, 1958, pp. 570–590; and Arendt, 'Understanding and Politics (The Difficulties of Understanding),' *Partisan Review*, 20:4, 1954, pp. 377–392. Arendt is well known for her *The Origins of Totalitarianism*, first published in 1951. The comment on infinite ends in Hegel is from Terry Pinkard, *Does History Make Sense? Hegel on the Historical Shapes of Justice*, Cambridge MA and London, 2017. Adorno's comment is found in his *History and Freedom: Lectures 1964-1965*, edited by Rolf Tiedemann, translated by Rodney Livingstone, Cambridge and Malden MA, 2009 [1964/65], p. 7. Also of interest for the role of the sublime in history is Polybius's criticism of the historian Phylarchus (third century B.C.). See his *The Rise of the Roman Empire*, II.54. Polybius warns his readers not to pursue a sensational effect by depicting sublime events. The step from the sublime to catharsis is less large than it might seem. Aristotle states that catharsis is the goal of tragedy in Chapter VI of his *Poetics*. He does this in a way that is later associated with the sublime. The tragedy arouses fear and pity in a way that causes catharsis: The reconciliation with existence. It struck me that in Aristotle's *Poetics*, 53b4–13, one already comes across Burke's definition of the sublime as a 'delightful horror'.

Chapter 8

For White, see his 'The Burden of History,' *History and Theory*, 5:2, 1966, pp. 111–134. For Guldi and Armitage, see their *The History Manifesto*, Cambridge, 2014. The argument that the historian is concerned with the past itself rather than with the present can be found in Johan Huizinga, *De wetenschap der geschiedenis*, Haarlem, 1937, for example on pp. 66, 92, and 96, and in Jo Tollebeek and Tom Verschaffel, *De vreugden van Houssaye. Apologie van de historische interesse*, Amsterdam, 1992. Both these works quote Burckhardt on the usefulness of history approvingly, respectively on p. 96 and p. 106. For Benjamin, see his posthumously published 'Theses on the Philosophy of History,' in Benjamin, *Illuminations*, London, 1999 [1955], pp. 245–255. The quotation of Michelet is taken from White, *Metahistory: The Historical Imagination in Nineteenth-Century Europe*.

List of Illustrations

Figure 5
Playing cards. Musée historique, Lausanne. Date: 1793.
Via Wikimedia Commons. © Public Domain   106

Figure 6
Angelus Novus. Artist: Paul Klee. Date: 1920. Oil
transfer and watercolour on paper, 31.8 × 24.2 cm. The
Israel Museum, Jerusalem. Object number: B87.0994.
© Public Domain   153

Recommended Readings

Allen, Amy, *The End of Progress: Decolonizing the Normative Foundations of Critical Theory*, New York, 2016.

Ankersmit, Frank, *Historical Representation*, Stanford, 2001.

Ankersmit, Frank, *Meaning, Truth, and Reference in Historical Representation*, Ithaca NY, 2012.

Bevernage, Berber, *History, Memory, and State-Sponsored Violence: Time and Justice*, New York, 2012.

Chakrabarty, Dipesh, *Provincializing Europe: Postcolonial Thought and Historical Difference*, Princeton, 2008 [2000].

Chartier, Roger, *On the Edge of the Cliff: History, Language, and Practices*, trans. Lydia Cochrane, Baltimore and London, 1997.

Crane, Susan, *Collecting and Historical Consciousness in Early Nineteenth-Century Germany*, Ithaca and London, 2000.

Fritzsche, Peter, *Stranded in the Present. Modern Time and the Melancholy of History*, Cambridge MA and London, 2004.

Gould, John, *Herodotus*, London, 1989.

Grafton, Anthony, *The Footnote: A Curious History*, Cambridge MA, 1997.

Grafton, Anthony, *What Was History? The Art of History in Early Modern Europe*, Cambridge, 2007.

Guldi, Jo and David Armitage, *The History Manifesto*, Cambridge, 2014.

Hughes-Warrington, Marnie, *History as Wonder: Beginning with Historiography*, New York, 2019.

Hunt, Lynn, *Writing History in the Global Era*, New York, 2014.

Jansen, Harry, *Hidden in Historicism: Time Regimes since 1700*, New York and London, 2020.

Kramer, Lloyd and Sarah Maza, eds., *A Companion to Western Historical Thought*, Malden MA and Oxford, 2002.

Kuukkanen, Jouni-Matti, *Postnarrativist Philosophy of Historiography*, Basingstoke, 2015.

LaCapra, Dominick, *Writing History, Writing Trauma*, Baltimore and London, 2001.

Lorenz, Chris, *Konstruktion der Vergangenheit. Eine Einführung in die Geschichtstheorie*, Cologne, 1997.

Marquard, Odo, *Zukunft braucht Herkunft. Philosophische Essays*, Stuttgart, 2003.

Momigliano, Arnoldo, *The Classical Foundations of Modern Historiography*, Berkeley and Los Angeles, 1990.

Morley, Neville, *Thucydides and the Idea of History*, London, 2014.

Paul, Herman, *Hayden White: The Historical Imagination*, Cambridge, 2011.

Peters, Rik, *History as Thought and Action: The Philosophies of Croce, Gentile, de Ruggiero and Collingwood*, Exeter, 2013.

Pinkard, Terry, *Does History Make Sense? Hegel on the Historical Shapes of Justice*, Cambridge MA and London, 2017.

Pomata, Gianna and Nancy Siraisi, *Historia: Empiricism and Erudition in Early Modern Europe*, Cambridge MA and London, 2005.

Pouncey, Peter, *The Necessities of War: A Study of Thucydides' Pessimism*, Rhinebeck, 2013.

Prüfer, Thomas, *Die Bildung der Geschichte. Friedrich Schiller und die Anfänge der modernen Geschichtswissenschaft*, Cologne, Weimar, and Vienna, 2002.

Roth, Paul, *The Philosophical Structure of Historical Explanation*, Evanston, 2020.

Spencer, Mark G., ed, *David Hume: Historical Thinker, Historical Writer*, University Park PA, 2013.

Tamm, Marek and Peter Burke, eds., *Debating New Approaches to History*, London and New York, 2018.

Trouillot, Michel-Rolph, *Silencing the Past: Power and the Production of History*, Boston, 1995.

Tucker, Aviezer, *Our Knowledge of the Past: A Philosophy of Historiography*, Cambridge, 2004.

Van den Akker, Chiel, *The Exemplifying Past: A Philosophy of History*, Amsterdam, 2018.

White, Hayden, *The Content of the Form: Narrative Discourse and Historical Representation*, Baltimore and London, 1987.

White, Hayden, *The Practical Past*, Evanston, 2014.

Woolf, Daniel, *A Global History of History*, Cambridge 2011.

Index